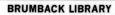

910094

780.92
GRE   vol 10
                             $25.90

Great Composers

910094
780.92   vol 10
GRE $25.90

Great Composers

THE BRUMBACK LIBRARY
OF VAN WERT COUNTY
VAN WERT, OHIO

THE
GREAT COMPOSERS
THEIR LIVES AND TIMES

A Beginner's Guide
to the
Opera

THE GREAT COMPOSERS
THEIR LIVES AND TIMES

A Beginner's Guide
to the
Opera

MARSHALL CAVENDISH
NEW YORK · LONDON · SYDNEY

Staff Credits

Editors
David Buxton BA (Honours)
Sue Lyon BA (Honours)

Art Editors
Debbie Jecock BA (Honours)
Ray Leaning BA (Honours),
PGCE (Art & Design)

Deputy Editor
Barbara Segall BA

Sub-editors
Geraldine Jones
Judy Oliver BA (Honours)
Nigel Rodgers BA (Honours), MA
Penny Smith
Will Steeds BA (Honours), MA

Designers
Steve Chilcott BA (Honours)
Shirin Patel BA (Honours)
Chris Rathbone

Picture Researchers
Georgina Barker
Julia Calloway BA (Honours)
Vanessa Cawley

Production Controllers
Sue Fuller
Steve Roberts

Secretary
Lynn Smail

Publisher
Terry Waters Grad IOP

Editorial Director
Maggi McCormick

Production Executive
Robert Paulley BSc

Managing Editor
Alan Ross BA (Honours)

Consultants
Dr Antony Hopkins
Commander of the Order
of the British Empire,
Fellow of the
Royal College of Music

Nick Mapstone BA (Honours), MA

Keith Shadwick BA (Honours)

Reference Edition Published 1990
Published by Marshall Cavendish Corporation
147 West Merrick Road
Freeport, Long Island
N.Y. 11520

Typeset by Walkergate Press Ltd, Hull, England
Printed and bound in Singapore by
Times Offset Private Ltd.

© Marshall Cavendish Limited MCMLXXXIV,
MCMLXXXVII, MCMXC
Library of Congress Cataloging-in-Publication Data

The Great composers, their lives and times.

Includes index.
1. Composers—Biography.   2. Music appreciation.
I. Marshall Cavendish Corporation.
ML390.G82   1987   780'.92'2 [B]   86-31294
ISBN 0-86307-776-5

ISBN 0-86307-776-5 (set)
0-86307-786-2 (vol)

Contents

Introduction

An opera is a drama in which the words, instead of being spoken as in a play, are all or partly sung, and are accompanied by music that is usually provided by an orchestra. At the same time, opera is a blend of many other art-forms, mixing drama, poetry, music, the visual arts and sometimes dance. It would seem that opera has something to offer everyone, and it has been described as encompassing the highest aspirations of the human spirit, but no other art-form – except perhaps modern painting and sculpture – has aroused such criticism, outrage and derision. Opera, it is said, is a blend of ludicrous plots, ridiculous conventions and over-the-top staging. These reactions are in the main the result of a lack of appreciation of opera's history and of changes in public taste. In the 20th century we expect realism in characters and plot, but 17th-century audiences were more interested in spectacular staging than in nuances of character and credibility of plot, while 18th-century opera-goers expected brilliant performances from rival singers, perhaps accounting for the much-derided operatic cliché of the dying character who sings at the top of his or her voice even when in the throes of death.

Criticisms of opera, though reasonable, are often unjustified. Other arts, like movies, plays and dance, depend for much of their impact on visual effects, and in many novels or plays the plot is contrived. In short, opera is much-misunderstood, and this volume seeks to correct the balance: it describes how opera developed during the Renaissance and how it has changed since then; it explains operatic conventions and provides a listener's guide to frequently performed operas; and gives a bibliography should you wish to know more about this most complex and potentially enjoyable of arts.

The Story of Opera

Chapter 1
The birth of opera

In Italy, around 400 years ago, a handful of Florentine artists laid the foundations for what was to develop into a colourful and spectacular form of entertainment – opera.

Opera – perhaps the most lavish of our cultural entertainments, with its rich combination of drama, music and the visual arts – has a long and fascinating history; a history that starts in Florence at the end of the 16th century and continues to the present day.

The story of opera, like all forms of art, is one of continual change and development. From its early beginnings in Italy, opera spread rapidly across Europe, becoming vastly popular as a public entertainment in the process. As it spread, each nation added its own chapter to the story and contributed its own style and characteristics, as composers and librettists reflected in their work certain schools of thought and even social and political events of the day. Consequently, a wealth of different national styles of opera emerged over the centuries, ranging from the elegantly stylized operas of the 18th century, through light-hearted comedies, to the spectacular and monumental tragedies of the 19th century – opera's 'Golden Age'.

The forerunners of opera

Opera's deepest roots stretch right back to the civilization of the ancient Greeks, who are known to have used music combined with drama in the enactment of their great tragedy plays. Dance and a chanting chorus of voices played a significant part too. Thus the Greeks brought together many of the basic elements of opera in raw form for the first time. Later, the Christian Church in Europe also made an important contribution. In the 13th and 14th centuries the church used drama, enlivened with music and singing, to communicate the Christian message to the illiterate masses.

Imagine an open-air stage erected in a market place outside a medieval cathedral, or in one of the great stone porches of a monastery, with a bible story being acted out by monks or travelling players. The singing would have been in single lines of chant, perhaps decorated with some instrumental accompaniment. These were the *Mystery Plays,* in Italy called *Sacre Rappresentazione,* which were a familiar part of medieval daily life, and another precursor to early opera in establishing a tradition of musically accompanied drama.

A further step forward can be found in the private entertainments commissioned by the wealthy families of late Renaissance Italy during the second half of the 16th century. Especially lavish events were put on to mark important occasions, like births and marriages, or to honour important guests. These were usually plays which included musical interludes – called *intermedi.*

The intermedi were wonderful spectacles in their own right and combined the best music of the day with the best of the visual arts. There were large instrumental ensembles, songs, madrigals and ballets performed against fantastic stage settings. Such was the popularity of the intermedi that more and more they came to dominate the plays they were accompanying. With their elements of music, drama and mythological themes, they provide another close link with early opera.

The Camerata

The elements of opera already present in the intermedi, were finally fused together, in the 1590s, into continuously sung drama by a group of Florentine scholars, poets and musicians known as the *Camerata.* The Camerata were members of the salon of Count Giovanni de' Bardi, a composer and patron of the arts in Florence. His salon, and later the houses of other patrons, Jacopo Corsi and Count Vernio, became the forum for discussions of all new artistic ideas. The Camerata began to react against the overwhelming extravagance of the intermedi, looking towards purer, more disciplined forms of expression. They wanted to restore what they saw as the superior aspects of Greek drama with its powerful simplicity and intensity, but recognized the importance of music in enhancing the emotions of

The intermedi (top, scene from a Medici court intermedi, 1589) were musical interludes in plays. With their stunning visual effects including lavish costumes (above) and elaborate stage sets the intermedi pointed the way to opera's spectacular combination of elements.

Medieval 'mystery plays' (left) – dramatized Bible stories accompanied by music and song – were among the forerunners of early opera.

characters in a drama. And it was out of their discussions that the leading members of the group – the composers Jacopo Peri and Guilio Caccini, the poet Ottavio Rinuccini and the singer and lutenist, Vincenzo Galilei (father of the great astronomer Galileo) – came to produce the earliest operas.

The invention of Recitative

It was Vincenzo Galilei who was largely responsible for helping the Camerata with the creation of a new musical narrative form called *recitative* – later to become an essential ingredient of all works of opera. Galilei had the idea that the spoken lines of the dramatic plot could be more effective than the usual plain verse if they were accompanied by music. He worked with Jacopo Corsi to produce examples of recitative in the form of single vocal lines with simple musical accompaniment.

The first work to be composed on these principles – and, effectively, the world's first opera – was *Dafne,* performed in 1598, at Corsi's house. The poet Ottavio Rinuccini wrote the words and Corsi and Jacopo Peri set them to music. Unfortunately, only fragments of *Dafne* remain. The earliest surviving opera is *Euridice,* also composed by Peri, with libretto again by Rinuccini, to honour the marriage of Maria de Medici and Henry IV of France. The first performance was on October 6 1600 at the Petti Palace in Florence. The work established a new flowing interchange between the different elements of ballet, music and drama, recitative, solo song and chorus music.

Orfeo – the first great opera

The revolutionary ideas of the Camerata, without doubt, produced works which laid the foundation stones for the future development of opera as a distinct art form, but their early compositions lacked the musical richness and inventiveness necessary to lift them to greatness. These operas consisted mainly of recitative, and must have sounded rather like the plainsong of monks. The musical accompaniment to the dramas was also very sparse, so all in all the works had little melodic interest. Indeed, these early works now seem a far cry from the modern idea of opera.

A few years later, however, a new composer emerged and produced what is generally recognized as the most important of all the early works and which, some would argue, marks opera's true beginning. His name was Claudio Monteverdi, the court musician to the Duke of Mantua, and his first opera *Orfeo* appeared in 1607. Not much is known about its first performance in Mantua but it is likely that the work was performed not in a theatre of any kind but in one of the small rooms used by the academicians for whom it was composed.

After *Orfeo,* Monteverdi went on to compose several more operas, culminating in his masterpiece *The Coronation of Poppea* (1642) which, along with *Orfeo* and *The Return of Ulysses to his Homeland* (1641) is still performed today.

Meanwhile, opera spread into all the major courts of Italy, from Tuscany to Lombardy, and south to Naples and Rome, where in the absence of a formal court, it was patronized by the wealthy members of the Vatican. With demand growing for larger public performances, the Teatro San Cassiano, the world's first public opera house with paid admission, opened in Venice in 1637. It opened with an opera called *Andromeda* by the composer Francesco Manelli and so popular did this and subsequent operas prove, that soon more than a dozen opera houses sprang up throughout the districts of Venice, until each area had its own rival theatre.

By this time, an increasing number of composers were becoming interested in the new art form. The most popular and influential among them was a composer named Pietro Francesco Cavalli, whose output of operas was prolific – between 1639 and 1666, he composed at least 40 – and he dominated the Venetian stage in the second half of the 17th century with his spectacular works.

Soon operas were being performed in all the major Italian cities to be enjoyed by nobility and general public alike – the first age of opera had begun in earnest.

Claudio Monteverdi (right) composed Orfeo *(title page below), the world's first great opera, in 1607. With this work he established the basic pattern for all future operas.*

Chapter 2
Italian Opera

In the 150 years following the birth of opera in Florence, Italy, and particularly Venice, remained the place where the seeds of opera grew and eventually bloomed into the most popular of all forms of entertainment.

With the opening of the first public opera house in 1637 – the Teatro San Cassiano, Venice – opera's social history began. Venice, the most cosmopolitan of all Italian cities, was the ideal place for this new form of entertainment to flourish and it soon became its centre. The city had a thriving trading population and an already fertile music tradition and the new trend was quick to catch on with the public. By 1700 opera was easily the most popular form of entertainment in Italy.

In fact, opera had little competition: 'straight' theatre hardly existed; cafe life did not come alive until the broad boulevards and gas lighting of the 19th century made it possible; and the soirées and the salons of London and Paris were yet to appear. Consequently, the opera houses not only provided entertainment, they became meeting places and social centres for a whole cross-section of the population. Attending the opera was a regular event not to be missed and the audiences as much as the performers played a role in helping the rise of opera.

The audiences of the 18th century
In years between the opening of the Teatro San Cassiano and 1700 it is known that at least fifteen more theatres sprang up in Venice alone, and opened their doors to the public. Meanwhile, opera was catching on elsewhere in Italy and soon many other cities had their own public opera houses.

The theatres had huge auditoriums, lined by uniform tiers of boxes set one above the other. The boxes were often hired by the season and some were even bought by families to be handed down through the generations. The compartments were not wide but they were deep, often with private rooms at the back. Ladies of 'uncertain character' occupied the lower boxes and assignations could be made with them during the performance. Indeed, they were so popular that the management sometimes let them in free as an added attraction. The upper boxes were usually occupied by the wealthier classes and were fitted out like drawing rooms, with comfortable sofas, draperies, valuables – and the inevitable card table. During the performance gentlemen would frequently ramble from one box to another for a game of *piquet* or *faro,* and the ladies – who knows what they got up to. It was customary to attend the opera masked and this, along with the darkness and background noise, provided ample cover for indiscretions.

Opera became hugely popular in 18th-century Italy – as popular as cinema would be later. Attendance at the opera was primarily a social event though, and despite the serious nature of the productions, the opera house would be abuzz with activity, including card playing, amorous liaisons and conversation, throughout performances (right). Full attention was reserved only for the best-loved arias and favourite scenes.

G. De Albertis 'L'Opera Seria' Museo Teatrale alla Scala, Milan

Galli-Bibiena 'Park with Castle Theatre Set' Archiv für Kunst und Geschichte

Italian baroque opera saw the development of spectacular stage effects, including stunning large scale set designs (below left and below). The monumental proportions of the sets provided an appropriate backdrop for the highly refined and elevated tone of the operas being played out on stage.

Anton Metastasio (right), sometimes called the Shakespeare of Italian opera, was the most famous librettist of the period and dominated opera seria for half a century. Some of his librettos were set to music as many as 60 to 70 times by different composers, among them, the young Mozart.

A greater contrast to the reverent attention paid by today's audiences can hardly be imagined. With gambling going on in the ante-rooms and hawkers touting refreshments and wares amongst the popular audience in the pit, the whole auditorium would be abuzz with activity throughout the performances. Foreign visitors to the opera houses remarked with amazement on the din against which the singers were supposed to perform. From this it may seem that the majority of the audience paid little attention to what was happening on the stage, but this was not the case. Audiences knew what they liked and were ready to respond with enthusiasm to a well-contrived dramatic situation or an outstanding aria. Popular taste, however, was guided by a group of *cognoscenti* – called the *abbati* – who decided which operas were to be hailed or booed, which singers were to be revered, and which arias should command the undivided attention of the thronging audience. Undeniably experts of opera, the abbati could also be the most ruthless critics, being able to spot every bit of plagiarism, faulty singing technique and even unorthodox violin bowing. They would make no secret of their judgements and took delight in exercizing their power in deciding the fate of the performers, rather like the ancient Romans' thumbs up or down at the Colisseum – and no one dared question their judgement.

Opera in 18th century Italy, therefore, was as popular as sport is today. In fact, so important was it that it became a kind of status symbol, the lavishness of productions reflecting the private wealth of individuals, towns and cities. Like the style of baroque architecture and painting prevalent at the time, opera was hugely elaborate and extravagant in

Operas of the Italian baroque period were mainly based on classical myths or heroic tales, yet were usually performed in contemporary costume (left). These looked especially incongruous alongside the mythological centaurs and sets (right), and yet it was not until much later that 'realistic' opera became the norm.

The huge, tiered auditoriums of the Italian opera houses, unlike their French counterparts of the same period, were generally dimly-lit to make the stage the main focus. The French, on the other hand, would often go to the opera, primarily to see and be seen.

Alessandro Scarlatti (1160–1725) (right), father of the great keyboard composer Domenico Scarlatti, was a key figure in operatic history. Through the 115 operas that he wrote during his life, he developed and elaborated the da capo aria and also the idea of 'dry' recitative. Both conventions were to have great influence on subsequent composers of opera.

its production. Vast sums of money had to be spent on stage effects and the star singers commanded enormous fees. They were lured from court to court, to be bid for, like football players today, and the funding of opera together with a dizzy refusal to consider cost effectiveness, drove many a princely sponsor to bankruptcy.

Despite their immense popularity at the time, only a small percentage of 17th and 18th century operas have survived to our day. Yet the output of the great Italian composers of the period, whose names are well known for other works, was prodigious – Alessandro Scarlatti wrote 115 operas, Vivaldi 40 and Pergolesi 13. But so much of their work has been lost – of Scarlatti's 115 operas, only 36 remain and only eight are in print.

The libretti – the opera scripts – on the other hand, are still with us. The vast majority were written by the celebrated poets Apostolo Zeno, Pietro Metastasio and Carlo Goldoni. Unlike the musical scores, the libretti were actually published in great numbers, since only by printing and selling their texts could the authors hope to make any money. Indeed, royalties from libretti were high, as Italian society expected to read the story of the operas and liked to get to know the most popular passages by heart. Once written, the texts were then used time and time again by different composers who set them to their own music. *Artaxerses* by Metastasio, for example, was set to music at least 45 times.

The first 'grand style' – Opera Seria

Librettos were all written to fit in with the very formalized notion of opera which was fashionable at the time. This meant classical and mythological subjects with heroic, moralistic, and, often, contorted plots. Stories were expected to be slotted into the same, extremely rigid pattern regardless of credi-

CASTRATI IN OPERA

The *castrato* phenomenon began, probably in medieval times, with a ban on women singing in church, a ban which lasted in Europe right until the 17th century. Consequently, castrated boys took the place of women in singing the higher parts. The tradition was continued in Italian opera, even though women were not actually debarred from the stage. In opera, the castrato soprano voice was prized as being more beautiful and purer than the female soprano – a little like a choirboy's but far stronger, with an enormous range, often up to an octave higher than a woman's voice.

Castrating pre-pubescent boys was technically illegal but the Church helped continue the practice by accepting castrated boys for choral singing and took the view that once done, it might as well profit from it by 'selling' their best castrati to the opera house. Many humble families in need of money did put their musical sons through the operation in the hope that they would become celebrated and affluent.

Boys who underwent the operation often did so unwittingly, and their parents had to explain away their condition as the result, for example, of being kicked by a horse or, even more unlikely, being pecked by a goose! Many castrati grew to statuesque height but they were often oddly proportioned with their heads being inordinately small compared with their bodies.

The last important composer of opera to write for the castrati voice was Meyerbeer, in his *Il Crociato in Egitto* (1824). The part was for Giovanni Battista Velluti (1780–1861) – the last great castrato. By the late 19th century, the phenomenon had become a social taboo and there was an attempt to conceal the identities of those that existed by alleging them to be falsettos and encouraging them to marry. The tradition did survive for a number of years in Roman Catholic churches and in 1913, the last professional castrato, Alessandro Moreschi, finally retired having made ten gramophone recordings between 1902–3.

---

bility. The plot's movement took place through recitative – sung blank verse accompanied for matter of fact remarks by a few chords on the harpsichord, or for more emotional statements, by the orchestra. But the elaborate arias took precedence above all. Each character was expected to sing three to five arias in a strict pecking order and no soloist could sing their second aria until everyone had had a turn at their first. Each aria represented a different emotion from the one immediately before it and this conveyed the inner meaning of the plot. No soloist expected to leave the stage without singing an important aria, nor could the singer stay on stage after finishing one. Some ensemble singing occurred but was not favoured by the soloists as they could not give full reign to their inventive powers. All this then, added up to the formalizing and standardizing of opera's structure, and from it emerged the first grand style – *opera seria,* or 'serious opera'.

The conventions of opera seria inevitably restricted the style of the librettists but the great librettists of the age found ways around the problems and prevented opera seria sinking deep into the ridiculous. Metastasio, for example, considerably reduced the absurdity of opera plots by purging the tragedies of incongruous comic elements, and generally restrained the extravagence of the special effects, but operas remained still far from naturalistic. Audiences saw nothing odd in the fact that a character about to take poison, or order a war,

17th century Italy saw the castrati *at the height of their popularity. The most famous was Carlo Broschi or 'Farinelli' (1705–1782) whose sweet voice so impressed King Philip V of Spain that he was employed by him for £3000 a year to cure his melancholia with singing.*

or be led off to death, should 'sing sweetly, quaver and calmly execute a pleasant and very long trill.'

Virtuoso singers – the darlings of the day

The truth was that the plot of the opera and the music were subservient to both the spectacle of the opera – the elaborate stage effects – and to the vanity of the singers. Composers were expected to serve the singer just as a song-writer now serves a pop star – the score was merely a base upon which singers could embellish and embroider. Only virtuosity captivated the audience and singers were judged by the imagination, taste and daring with which they departed from the score. They could change key at will, leaving the hapless orchestra (or more often, the composer at the keyboard) to improvise.

A famous story of the great castrato singer Farinelli, shows the indulgent lengths singers would go to in order to impress an audience, and relates how he and the trumpet player accompanying his aria, rivalled each other in a display of competitive virtuosity. Eventually the trumpeter, out of breath, gave up, thinking the singer would also draw battle, 'when Farinelli, with a smile upon his countenance, shewing he had only been sporting all that time, broke out all at once in the same breath with fresh vigour and not only swelled and shook the note, but ran the most difficult and rapid divisions and was at last silenced only by the acclamations of the audience'.

Farinelli's fame was prodigious; he even came to England, where he was immensely popular and earned the fantastic sum, for those days, of £5,000 in a season. He had an almost legendary career and was as great a figure of the 18th century as Liszt and Paganini were of the next century.

With Farinelli, and the pre-eminence of the soloist voice in *opera seria,* the strange Italian institution of the *castrato* peaked. The vocal powers of the castrato were so amazing (Farinelli could sing three octaves with comfort) that women were often given subordinate or less interesting roles and it was the castrati who were the glittering stars of the age. The path to the top, however, was not easy and only a relatively small number actually attained the heights of stardom. The boys who underwent the operation often came from poor families and they were either sold – effectively into 'musical slavery' – direct to a music institute or parents would pay for them to study under individual music masters. Others were sent to the *conservatorios* – music schools. Pupils were trained in extensive vocal acrobatics and were expected to have a thorough grasp of musical theory. There were a prescribed number of ways in which a theme could be embellished and they had to know them all. The daily study routine involved two hours of singing practice and four hours of theory and letters, which was the study of words and how to bring out their meaning. Of those that began the training, many fell by the wayside, either because they lacked the musical talent necessary, or because their voices did not live up to expectations; the rest made their stage début between the ages of 15 to 20, captivating audiences with their youthful beauty.

Many castrati lived normal, ordinary lives – some were even famous lady-killers – but the Church did not allow them to marry. Others were decidedly effeminate and dressed in women's clothing both on and off-stage.

The Intermezzi

In spite of the seeming absurdity of men dressed as women and playing female roles, the operas of this period were intensely earnest. In fact, spectacular ballet troupes, or teams of soliders or fencers for realistic battle scenes, were usually brought in to give some visual relief. But it was the *intermezzi,* the comic scenes between the acts of opera seria, which breathed a lighter breath of air into performances. These, in complete contrast to the epic drama of the main opera, were humorous scenes between two characters and invariably inspired by everyday life. The appeal of these little comic interludes began to grow in their own right, becoming eventually, a stepping stone for the rise of comic opera, or *opera buffa,* in Italy after 1760 – the classical period.

In the meantime, opera was beginning to spread abroad, notably to France where it was imported by young Louis XIV's Chief Minister, Cardinal Mazarin. The French did not immediately take to the new Italian entertainment but they soon moulded a style to suit their own taste. The age of Baroque Opera in France was to see some of the most spectacular productions of all time.

The intermezzi, *or comic interludes between the acts of Italian serious opera, must have been something akin to our modern-day 'situation comedies'. Characters, unlike those in the main dramas, were drawn from everyday life, with domestic misunderstandings, between master and servant or husband and wife (right), invariably providing the main source of humour. The great popularity of these comic scenes was to herald the rise of comic opera in its own right.*

School of Longhi 'Intermezzo' Museo Teatrale alla Scala, Milan/Scala

Chapter 3

Opera comes to France

As opera spread outwards from its Italian birthplace most countries happily inherited the Italian tradition. Not so the French, though, who formed their own distinctive style.

After its beginnings and rapid rise in Italy, opera was soon in great demand abroad. The Italians were already the acknowledged masters of the art and the talents of the best Italian artists were eagerly imported by foreign courts keen to feast on this rich new entertainment. Everywhere audiences were enraptured by the rich musicality, the virtuoso singing and the lavish productions of Italian opera. Everywhere, that is, except France.

When opera first arrived in France in the 1640s, brought to the Royal court of Louis XIV by his Chief Minister, Cardinal Mazarin, it was not the unbounded success it had been elsewhere in Europe – particularly in Austria and the many independent German states, where the Italian style was whole-heartedly accepted. This was partly due to personal opposition to Mazarin (an Italian himself) who had created anti-Italian feeling by being a foreigner in a position of power, and through his patronage of the Venetians; partly because the French already had their own tradition of spectacular entertainment in the form of the *ballet de cour* (court ballet).

The vogue for dance had begun some 60 years previously with a magnificent court entertainment mounted in 1581 by the Dowager Queen, Catherine de Medici – the *Ballet Comique de la Reine*. In this, the first of the court ballets, dance was mixed with spectacular stage effects, music, singing and poetry to such great effect that it became the predominant form of entertainment. It also began a taste for the inclusion of ballet in other entertainments too.

This love of dance was reinforced by the King, for Louis XIV had a marked penchant for dance himself and enjoyed showing off his elegant deportment by taking part in performances. At the age of 14, he had appeared in the *Ballet de la Nuit* (1653), in a glittering costume of fiery rays, as the Sun King – the title by which he was known ever afterwards. However, it was not only the lack of dance in Italian opera that the French missed, they also found the Italian music over-heavy with emotion and too florid for their refined aristocratic tastes. Nonetheless, opera got a foothold in Paris by the 'sweetening' of the native Italian product with specially included ballet and plenty of spectacular stage effects.

Mechanical wonders of the stage

Those operas that did kindle some interest in Paris,

Louis XIV (1638-1715) – The Sun King (right) – dominated the arts in France throughout his long reign. His personal love of dance, particularly ballet, strongly influenced the development of a distinct French style of opera.

Jean Baptiste Lully (above, with his musicians), gave France its own national operatic style which was quite distinct from the Italian tradition – tragédie-lyrique.

owed much to the spectacular effects achieved with the Venetian stage machinery. The outstanding stage manager of the period was Giacomo Torelli, brought to France from Venice by Mazarin. He astonished French audiences with the sight of houses blazing on stage, mountains moving and cloud-borne choirs descending from on high. So popular were these marvels of the stage, that Paris soon had its own Theatre of Machines, built in 1660 in the Tuileries and a taste for the spectacular would become a firm feature, not only of future French opera but of their theatre in general.

The effects that could be achieved by the skilled craftsmen and designers must have been truly fantastic, surpassing anything attempted on the theatre stage today. Heavenly visions of moving 'cloud chariots', on occasions large enough to carry up to forty people, could glide across a backdrop of layers of clouds in perpetual motion, all shimmering with innumerable hidden lights. Huge palaces could be lowered on to the stage or made to 'float' in mid-air, glittering and dazzling with tinsel and gold while whole dance troupes made their entrances and exits on moving machines. All these effects relied on complex systems of brass wires, pulleys, ropes, beams and platforms and of course, the ingenuity of the Italians. Another special effect that the Italians loved to create was that of blazing buildings on stage. For this they used flame coloured canvas stretched over iron girders with flickering torches placed behind. When supplemented with sparks and smoke

and real controlled flames, together with the sound of beams crashing to the ground, audiences were sometimes so taken by fright that they would be ready to leap from their seats and run away. All these effects, with the addition of their own ballet, gradually seduced the French to accept opera. Eventually, in the 1670s, France gave birth to a style of its very own.

Lully – Father of French opera

Opera's founder in France was a protegé of the King, the remarkable and ruthless Jean Baptiste Lully, ironically, yet another Italian.

His career is a classic success story. Giovanni Battista Lulli (1632–87), the son of a miller, was born in Florence. At the age of 14 he was brought to France by the Duke of Lorraine and placed in the service of Louis XIV's cousin, Mlle de Montpensier, who wanted a partner for Italian conversation. Before long Lulli changed his name to the more French 'Jean-Baptiste Lully', picked up a musical education in the course of his service and showed such talent as a violinist that Mlle de Montpensier put him in charge of her musical entertainments. In 1652, when she was banished from the court into rural exile, Lully stayed on in Paris, the following year performing in the *Ballet de la Nuit* alongside the young King, whom he tactfully coached for his part. He won Louis' favour, and from then on was careful to keep a firm hold on it, displaying a dazzling array of talents as dancer, singer, intrumentalist,

Pure Italian opera did not suit the French. Consequently, they took the elements they liked most – namely dance and spectacular stage effects – and exaggerated them in operas of their own. Huge extravaganzas were enacted in the open air (left) or in theatres. Stage machinery, often on an enormous scale – like this system (right) designed to imitate a storm-tossed ship – was used to breathtaking effect. Even the centaurs (below, left) which made frequent appearances due to the classical plots, had workable rear legs for realistic effect. Ballet was an essential ingredient of Lullian opera with dancers playing a dramatic, as well as decorative, role. French baroque opera, like its Italian counterpart, was mostly performed in elaborate forms of contemporary costume (below and below right). This costume design for a male dancer, below, possibly represents Louis XIV as a young man.

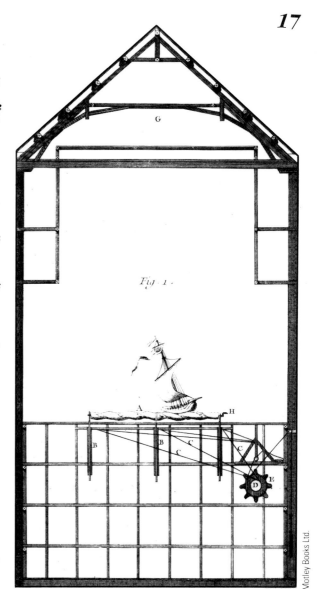

composer and director.

As well as changing his name, Lully also became thoroughly French in musical outlook. In the 1650s he composed a series of highly successful ballets, and during 1660–62 emerged as the victor in a kind of symbolic contest between French and Italian tastes. When the splendid operas *Xerxes* and *Ercole Amante*, by the famous Francesco Cavalli, were to be staged for the King, Lully was commissioned to provide ballets between all the acts (evidently Louis found the prospect of unadulterated Italian opera quite intolerable). In the event, while the actual operas were indifferently received, Lully's entr'actes won great admiration. Cavalli, disillusioned by this musical injustice, went back to Italy, and Italian opera was not heard in France for some years.

By this time, Lully's fortune was made. He was appointed Master of the King's Music in 1661, and formally took French nationality. A year later he began a partnership with the great playwright, Molière, which produced a string of comedy-ballets.

Lully included many semi-operatic elements in his ballets, giving increasing prominence to the vocal and instrumental parts but as yet had never attempted true opera. Finally, others were to take the first step – and Lully was to reap the benefit.

The birth of French opera

The first French challenge to Italian opera came with the collaboration of dramatist Pierre Perrin and composer Robert Cambert. In 1669, the Académie Royale de Musique (later known as l'Opéra) was set up by Louis XIV and Perrin was granted a three year licence to control it. Two years later, in 1671, Perrin and Cambert produced what is generally regarded as the first French opera, *Pomone,* and though not very dramatic, it was operatic in that it was sung all the way through. It was staged with great success and this may well have aroused Lully's jealousy. With Perrin in gaol, thanks to the machinations of two unscrupulous managers, Lully took his opportunity. He bought the licence from the desperate Perrin and took complete control of music for the French theatre. His first opera, *Cadmus et Hermione* (1673) delighted Louis so much that he gave Lully's Académie Royale de Musique a permanent home in the Palais-Royal.

Lully, like the Sun King, brooked no rivals. From then on, his were the only operas performed. After *Cadmus,* he enjoyed a succession of triumphs that went on to the very end of his career. This, however, was cut short by a trivial accident: Lully was in the habit of conducting his orchestra by beating time on the floor with his staff. One day, whilst conducting a rehearsal, he inadvertently jabbed his staff into his foot, causing blood poisoning and an infection that led to his death.

The new French tradition

Lully's operas, which he called *tragédies-lyriques,* created a distinctively French style that lasted with relatively little change for a century.

The *tragédie-lyrique* was prefaced by a short overture, followed by a prologue, whose purpose was simply to lavish flatteries on the monarch. The subject matter was always solemn and grand, consisting of knightly romances or classical myths. But despite the emphasis on spectacle and ballet, their drama was much more tightly structured and emotionally cooler than their Italian counterparts.

Even after Lully's death the *tragédie-lyrique* kept

its dominant position, reaching its culmination with Jean-Phillipe Rameau (1683–1764). After working as cathedral organist in provincial towns, Rameau came to Paris at the age of 40 and soon became known as a theorist, a much sought-after teacher, and a composer of pieces for the harpsichord.

Rameau's first *tragédie-lyrique, Hippolyte et Aricie* was performed at the Palais Royal in October 1733. This, and such later operas as *Castor et Pollux* (1737) and *Dardanus* (1739) divided Parisians into two camps – enthusiastic 'Ramistes' and conservative 'Lullistes'. For although Rameau followed many of the operatic conventions laid down by Lully, he outraged the orthodox by the complexity and over-sensuous quality of his music. However, it was not long before Rameau had overcome all opposition and, by 1745, he was appointed court composer to Louis XV.

A challenge to tragedy

Then, towards the end of Rameau's life, the first signs appeared of a more radical shift in taste and feeling. In 1752 a performance of *La Serva Padrona,* a comic intermezzo by the Italian composer Pergolesi, took Parisian audiences by storm. This heralded a revolution in French opera, which eventually swept away the Baroque traditions of Lully and Rameau to make way for a new vogue for comedy in France.

Meanwhile in Italy, the popularity of the ornate and artificial serious opera was already fading in favour of a new and vivacious comic style. Centred in Naples, *opera buffa* as it was called, had its appeal in a refreshing naturalness of human emotion and day-to-day situations and it was poised to take opera's story into a new era. Once again, Italy led the way.

Rameau by Carmontelle. Musée Chantilly/Bulloz

Lully's illustrious successor, the composer Jean-Philippe Rameau (left), like Lully, maintained a French style of opera. Towards the end of his life, however, there was a move in a new direction: Pergolesi's comic intermezzo La Serva Padrona, *performed in Paris in 1752, took audiences by storm and sparked off the famous 'War of the Buffoons'. In this the philosopher Jean-Jacques Rousseau attacked Rameau, proclaiming the supremacy of Italian spontaneity, melody and truth to nature – values which were eventually to set the French back on the road to re-adopting Italian opera.*

Chapter 4

Opera Buffa

***Down-to-earth and light-hearted, opera buffa –
essentially the comedy of wit and manners – burst
upon the world from the stages of Naples, and Italy
again led the way in the creation of a brand new style.***

Opera seria, the first grand style of opera, dominated the European scene for over one hundred years following its establishment in Venice in the mid 17th century. But while opera seria ruled the roost during this period, and even clung on as a popular style until the 1790s, a rival style emerged, again in Italy, that by 1750 led the world of opera in a new and exciting direction. This was comic opera or – to give it its Italian name – *opera buffa.*

Opera buffa's brand of down-to-earth wit and social satire was to prove so revolutionary that its repercussions were eventually felt not only all through Italy, but out beyond its borders, prompting composers across Europe to try their hand at this new Italian style. And this style was to find its ultimate expression in the great classic buffa operas, such as Rossini's *Barber of Seville* and Mozart's *Marriage of Figaro.*

A background of comedy

Comedy in opera was not exactly new. Monteverdi had included comic servants and other farcical characters in his early classical dramas. His successor, too, Francesco Cavalli, the prolific composer who dominated the Venetian opera stage in the late 17th century, had also used a comic element as light relief in his high tragedies. This continued until Metastasio saw fit to purge all tragic works of any incongruous humour or farce to create operas with an unequivocally serious tone – opera seria. Any humour was then banished from the opera proper to the *intermezzi* between the acts.

But even before the appearance of the intermezzi, comedy existed as a separate form of entertainment in its own right – as the *Commedia dell'arte.* This popular style of improvised comedy play, with its set of stock character types performed by troupes of travelling actors throughout Europe, was to provide the inspiration for a fresh style of opera.

In the first decades of the 18th century, some of the Commedia characters became associated with regional dialects, especially in the theatrical circles around Naples, prompting writers to produce whole comedies in dialect. This use of dialect, local character and local humour became the trademark of the Neapolitan comic style. And it was in Naples that the seeds of comedy and opera first grew together.

***The works of composer Francesco Cavalli
(1602–1676), organist in the Cathedral of St Mark's,
Venice (left), contained sparks of humour which
pointed the way to the development of Italian comic
opera – opera buffa.***

Carlo Goldoni (above) was the brilliant Venetian playwright and librettist who developed basic comic opera into a more refined form of social comedy, and this helped make it popular throughout Europe. His works provided inspiration for countless composers, including Vivaldi, Piccinni and Haydn.

Mauro Pucciarelli

Naples, birthplace of opera buffa

Alessandro Scarlatti, the great composer of opera seria, was largely responsible for the establishment of Naples as the operatic centre of Italy – in the first half of the 18th century. Through Scarlatti's influence, students of music from all over Italy flocked to the conservatorios of Naples rather than Venice – where opera had begun – and Naples became a thriving theatrical centre. At first mainly Venetian and Roman operas were performed there, but soon Neapolitan composers began to develop their own individual style. Then, in 1709, one of the theatres in Naples put on the first opera buffa and it proved so successful that regular seasons of comic opera continued. Comic opera did not exactly spread by leaps and bounds immediately though – the highly serious plots of opera seria predominated in popularity in most theatres and did so for many years. But the clownish buffa style flourished, especially in the form of the *intermezzi,* and in these the Neapolitans excelled.

One intermezzo, in particular, was destined to capture the imagination of audiences wherever it was performaed. This was Pergolesi's *La Serva Padrona* (The Maid as Mistress) which was first performed in Naples in 1733. It encapsulated all the elements of Neapolitan opera buffa in a high spirited inter-act comedy, written to be performed along with the composer's opera seria *Il Prigioner Superbo.* The main opera has long since been forgotten, but its intermezzo lives on as a timeless work, as fresh today as when it was first written.

La Serva Padrona relates the story of a cunning young maidservant called Serpina who manages to get the better of her old and foolish master, Uberto, to become mistress of his house and his wealth. With the help of an accomplice (another servant, who is the only non-speaking character and whose comedy arises solely out of mime) Serpina tricks Uberto into marrying her and thus elevates her status to lady of the house.

This short work contains, in distilled form, all the characteristics of opera buffa, both musical and dramatic – such as the sending up of human foibles, whether stupidity, vanity, miserliness or affectation, by an underling who through quick wit or common sense, invariably triumphs in the end. These elements proved to be the essence of opera buffa's success, and it is easy to see why. Opera, which had been formerly confined to the remote and mystical settings of opera seria, was suddenly brought closer to home, and more importantly, to within the actual experience of its audiences. Characters were no longer the kings and queens of classical mythology, instead they were ordinary folk – business men,

---

THE COMMEDIA DELL'ARTE

The Italian *Commedia dell'arte* was a form of improvised comedy of masks (the players all wore masks) that flourished between the mid-16th and mid-17th centuries, achieving huge popularity and fame through France, Germany, Spain and even England and Russia. Its characters and plots had a great influence on the development of drama and, therefore, on opera too – many direct descendents being especially evident in the plots of opera buffa. The Commedia plays were not written plays, but relied totally on the skill of the actors and their ability to improvise comedy. They followed only skeletal scenarios, which they embellished with ad-libbed routines, virtuoso displays of mime and acrobatics and at times, songs.

The plots were varied but always included a selection of stock characters and almost invariably revolved round the trials and tribulations of a pair of young lovers. A series of farcical situations, cases of mistaken identity, confusion and disguise would inevitably ensue before the lovers could be united in a happy ending.

The main characters, known as the *zanni,* consisted of a number of stock types – and several of them can be directly linked with the types which later appeared, in more refined form in opera. There was *Pantalone,* the Venetian merchant, the archetypal lascivious old man, who could also be the jealous guardian of his daughter, the love-sick *Inamorata.* Pantalone's crony was *il Dottore,* the doctor, a bumbling and pedantic Bolognese lawyer. Another popular figure was *Colombina,* the cheeky maidservant, or artful confidant of the *Inamorata.* There was also a whole host of others, the agile *Arlecchino* (Harlequin), the cunning *Brighella,* and *Scapino,* the coward. *Pedrolino* was the origin of the mournful Pierrot figure of 19th century French theatre, and *Pulcinella,* the English 'Punch'. All the characters were well-known by the audiences, recognizable by their standardized masks and costumes, but even more so by their predictable personalities.

Among the many playwrights to be influenced by the genre were Shakespeare and also Molière and Beaumarchais. France also began its own version of the Commedia which in turn, contributed to the development of France's own opéra comique.

Der poßierliche und zu aller Recreation fertig Scaramuz.

Facetiarum ille Magister, quem Itali Scar vocant.

Pergolesi's La Serva Padrona *(The Maid as Mistress; title page right) first performed in 1733, became the most famous of all Neapolitan comic intermezzi. Its tuneful melodies and lively wit made it a model for the many full-length comic operas that were to follow.*

Scaramuccio, Mezzetino and Arlequino (below, from left to right) three of the numerous and familiar stock characters from Commedia dell'arte. The actors playing Commedia characters wore standardized masks and costumes – like Harlequin's coloured, diamond-patterned suit – so that audiences would immediately recognize the role they were to play.

artisans, servants and the like – all recognizable types whose wit, repartee and comical intrigue kept audiences blissfully amused.

In common with the well-known Commedia tradition, characters evolved into certain stock types, but in spite of the set patterns that inevitably emerged, opera buffa remained a lively genre, always adaptable to new and topical modes of satire with a diversity and lively humour, ranging from slapstick to elegant witticisms. The parody of its rival opera seria could, needless to say, be particularly devastating. But although Italian serious opera remained popular in the face of the challenge from

opera buffa, and was to do so, in fact, right up until the 1790s, it was not long before interest in the new style of opera spread to other Italian cities.

Carlo Goldoni's 'comedy of character'

By the 1760s in Italy opera buffa had developed into polished, full-length social comedy. This was first achieved in Venice, mainly through the efforts of one man, the eminent playwright Carlo Goldoni (1707–1793). As well as being an important reformer of spoken drama, Goldoni had a profound effect on the course of musical comedy and can be credited with its subsequent huge rise in popularity.

A few years after the arrival of the first Neapolitan opera buffa in Venice in 1743, Goldoni produced his own Venetian brand of comic opera in collaboration with the composer Baldassare Galuppi. This was the start of a whole series of comedies which took the standard characters of the Commedia dell'arte tradition and injected them with new life so that they became refined and rounded characters, who expressed themselves through witty dialogue, rather than by improvized action and cliched situations. With Goldoni, nuance of character was expertly handled and he used it to expose and ridicule human nature. The result was social satire – brilliant comedy on the morals and manners of the Venetian society in Goldoni's day. In his plays and libretti, Goldoni also managed to break out of the commedia-type mould, with its impossible coincidences and

Gioacchino Rossini carried 18th century opera buffa forward into the Romantic age. His operas, many of which are represented on this souvenir fan, shown above, enjoyed great popularity when they appeared – even if, in many ways, they were the anachronistic survivors of a former classical age.

clumsy ironies – the action became speedy, plots more straightforward.

In short, Goldoni's libretti represented a highly developed form of opera buffa and, for the most part, the innovations he made proved highly popular. By the time he died, Goldoni had produced no less than 250 plays and libretti, a valuable legacy which provided a mainstay for operatic composers for over 50 years.

The Italian influence

Towards the end of the century, opera buffa was having an increasing impact abroad. In 1782, Paisiello finished his setting of *The Barber of Seville* – a delightful opera based on the first of a trilogy of plays by Beaumarchais (later overtaken in popularity by Rossini's version of the work). The libretto, translated into Italian, offered the composer a rich foundation for subtle characterization as well as high comedy. Although first seen in St Petersburg, it was also produced in Paris in 1784 where it made a profound impression. By November 1785, Mozart and his librettist Lorenzo da Ponte were also busy working on an Italian libretto based on the second play of the trilogy, *The Marriage of Figaro*. The work was premiered in Vienna in the spring of 1786 and has been an example of the highest level of musical comedy ever since, where tragi-comic elements are mingled with traditional opera buffa verve to produce a lively and entertaining work of great sensitivity.

Mozart then, took the formula of Italian comic opera and pushed it to its limits. He raised, what can only be called farcical stories, to levels of great art and universal appeal, by his deft drawing of character and haunting orchestration.

In Mozart's comedies – he wrote seven opera buffa in all, but two were unfinished – the influences of the Italian commedia tradition remain strong. The plots contain all the improbable situations, mistaken identities and coincidences of these travelling plays. Several of his characters too, are direct descendents

of the stock Commedia types, such as Despina, the maid and voice of good sense in *Cosi fan Tutte,* Leporello, the lazy comic servant in *Don Giovanni* and Bartolo, the bad-tempered doctor figure of *Figaro.* His plots, like those of the Commedia, taken at face value, seem to border on the ridiculous. But Mozart's emphasis is on character, rather than plot, and it is here that his genius shines. Mozart's characters are drawn with a masterly intuition of human nature together with an innate sense of the fragile balance between the comedy and tragedy of life – and all expressed through music. It is not surprising that they have become some of the best loved classics of all time.

Along with Mozart's comedies, another masterpiece of Italian opera buffa, still frequently performed in opera houses all over the world, is Rossini's *The Barber of Seville.* In many ways Rossini may be seen as the culmination of opera buffa and the classical era in Italy. His successors, Donizetti and Verdi immersed themselves in the romantic movement sweeping Europe in the 19th century – opera's golden age.

Paralleling opera buffa's rise in Italy, and its popularity abroad, was a movement in France towards musical comedy. The new Italian comedies arrived in France at a time when old values were already under fire by the leading philosophers of the day, notably Jean-Jacques Rousseau. He welcomed Italian opera buffa as an example of 'truth to nature' and 'spontaneity' – two dictates of the new Age of Enlightenment in France. Rousseau's influence was such that the second half of the 18th century eventually saw the decline of France's tradition of highly artificial and serious *tragédies-lyriques* as laid down by Lully and Rameau. And against this background of changing social values, as well as the influence of Italian opera buffa, and the native French farces of the traditional fairs of Paris with their popular *vaudeville* songs, there emerged an individual French style of comic opera – *opéra comique.*

Chapter 5

Opéra Comique

*Taking a cue from the lively opera buffa of Italy,
the great philosopher Jean-Jacques Rousseau
championed the cause of a new, light French style
– opéra comique.*

*The **Théâtres de la Foire** (Fair theatres), part of the great 18th-century fairs held in Paris, were the birthplace of opéra comique.
The open air performances, like the one shown above, had all the elements of the first French comic operas – stock characters, lively satire and popular vaudeville songs.*

French serious opera, tragédie-lyrique, reigned supreme in France from the 1670s, when it began, for a good 80 years. Around the middle of the 18th century, though, its popularity faded fast as a lighter, simpler form of opera took its place – *opéra comique*. Influenced by the Italian style of comic opera (opera buffa) that was rivalling opera seria in Italy, the move towards opéra comique was also helped by the changing view of society as expressed by the great French philosophers of the day – the philosophers of the Age of Enlightenment – namely Jean-Jacques Rousseau, Diderot and Voltaire. With Rousseau as its main exponent, opéra comique was a direct product of the new social climate in France,

but it also owed much to the arrival of Italian opera buffa and to the traditional Fair theatres of Paris.

The birth of opéra comique

The beginnings of French comic opera can be traced to the great annual fairs of Paris which themselves dated back to the Middle Ages. The most important were the *Foire de Saint-Germain,* which was held in early spring, and the summer *Foire de Saint-Laurent.* The fairs were like huge markets where agricultural produce, livestock and all kinds of merchandise were brought to be sold. In among the market trading, sideshows with acrobats, jugglers and all sorts of curiosities competed for the attention of customers.

Over a long period, some of the sideshows developed into theatrical entertainments with music, and, as the open air stalls eventually turned into a permanent covered market, so the theatrical entertainments had their own permanent booths. These were the *Théâtres de la Foire* where the French players gave their version of the Commedia dell'arte comedies, with similar stock characters which appeared over and over again. Music also had its role in the plays in the form of popular tunes, or *vaudevilles* as they were called, which could be fitted with new words to suit different situations.

As the fairground theatres gained popularity, the established bodies such as the Académie Royale de Musique (the Opéra) and the Comédie-Francaise began to see them as a threat. With the help of royal support which granted them a legal monopoly, they made strenuous efforts to enforce their sole right to

J. L. Charmet

perform sung and spoken drama. The fairs, in turn, did their best to get round these laws. When at first actors were forbidden to appear in dialogue, they switched to monologues – as one actor spoke, another replied in mime and gesture. Then players found their right to speak taken away, so, with special permission from the Opéra, they sang their plays instead. Then, when singing was banned, the ingenious actors used the voices of their audiences, lowering banners over the stage with song words written on them, and, as the audiences sang, the actors mimed their plays.

These vaudeville plays, against all odds, became extremely popular and at the Foire de Saint-Germain in 1715 were billed as *opéras comiques*. But still, the battle between establishment and fringe continued; in fact, it lasted right up until the mid-century when the plays were legitimized. Rivalry was often expressed through parody and the Fair theatres frequently sent up the artificiality of tragédie-lyrique.

By contrast with tragédie-lyrique, and Italian comic opera (opera buffa), the opéras comiques had dialogue-passages which were not sung, but spoken unaccompanied, a distinguishing feature that was to

Painting by Dunouy, Musee Marmottan, Oaris. J. L. Charmet

Jean-Jacques Rousseau (1712–78), writer, composer and philosopher, (left), was a leading figure in the famous journalistic row of the mid 18th century – the **Querelle des Bouffons**. *This centred on the relative virtues of French versus Italian music. Rousseau (depicted in the above painting, contemplating the beauty of nature), idealized the 'natural' and saw Italian music as more spontaneous and 'natural' than the heavy, ornate French baroque style. After two years of heated debate, Rousseau's view prevailed, causing the decline of tragédie-lyrique and heralding the rise of opéra-comique.*

remain into the 19th century. Although, at first, the music of the vaudeville plays was not particularly sophisticated, the simple tunes eventually grew into *ariettes,* a compromise between the popular song and the learned aria. Much of the appeal of opéra comique was in the dialogue however, which was always witty and pointed.

The quarrelsome Rousseau
In the early 1750s, the evolution of opéra comique and the decline of tragédie-lyrique was decisively influenced by the radical thinking of France's leading intellectuals, most notably that of Jean-Jacques Rousseau (1712–78). Tragédie-lyrique was historically remote in terms of its subject material, as well as highly complex and almost ludicrously ornate. It was also out-dated in that the operas were also intended to glorify the French monarchy. But by 1750, the unpopular and dissolute reign of Louis XV had left the royal image badly tarnished. At the same time, brilliant writers such as Voltaire, Diderot and Rousseau were launching scathing attacks on the established order and its values. Between them they expressed a radically different view of life in which the ordinary man and woman, not just nobles and heroes, were important, and truth to nature, simplicity and sincerity became values to admire rather than to scoff at.

Rousseau's philosophical writings idealized 'nature' and denounced the corruptions of civilization, making a cult of simple, spontaneous feeling. For him, Italian opera buffa was the embodiment of his ideals and as an amateur composer and musical journalist he was able to put his theories into practice and argue their worth.

In 1752 he composed a short opéra comique called *Le Devin du Village.* (The Village Soothsayer),

Rousseau's short opéra-comique, Le Devin du Village *(The Village Soothsayer) (1752), was his most successful and influential musical work. After the artificiality of the baroque style, Rousseau sought to reflect his ideas of simple melodies and 'naturalness' through the romantic sentiments of ordinary country characters (below).*

which was performed before the royal family at Fontainebleau, and then in Paris at the Opéra. There was nothing earth-shattering about Rousseau's music, but the piece was warmly received because its sentimental love story, peasant hero and heroine, and simple melodies were just what people had been waiting for. The work was a complete departure from tragédie-lyrique and became very influential starting a trend for the pastoral scene in opera.

Rousseau's opera appeared shortly after an Italian company had created a sensation with their performances of Pergolesi's comic intermezzo, *La Serva Padrona* (The Maid as Mistress) in the summer of 1752. The reception of Italian comedy was another sign that times were changing since the same intermezzo had gone unnoticed when performed in the French capital only a few years earlier. Now Parisian audiences, tired of the baroque grandeur and solemn divinities of tragedie-lyrique, were swept away by the lively, tuneful music and earthy characters of the Italian opera buffa.

The success of the comic Italian players, or *bouffons* (from which we derive the word, buffoon) gave impetus to a row which had recently broken out over the rival merits of Italian and French music. The *Querelle des Bouffons* (The War of the Buffoons) was the name given to the pamphlet war which raged between the opposing parties, as article after article was published to argue the case of one over the other. The debate flared up still more fiercely when Rousseau dared to attack the great contemporary master of tragédie-lyrique, Jean-Philippe Rameau. Rameau himself then entered the

The German composer, Christoph Willibald Gluck (above) was, after Monteverdi, opera's second founder. In tune with the radical views of the 18th-century French intellectuals, Gluck advocated that beauty of expression lay in simplicity, and in his serious operas he pruned away superfluous florid embellishments and set opera on a new path where the drama became as important as the music.

fray, and between 1753–54 the *Querelle* generated intense public interest. Rousseau argued, with more eloquence than logic, for the inherent and absolute superiority of Italian as a sung language – evidently undeterred by the fact that he himself had written an opera in French – but the main battle was fought over the relative importance of harmony and melody, in other words, the 'artificial' versus the 'natural'. For Rameau, harmony was the foundation of musical excellence. Rousseau dismissed it as a decadent over-refinement.

The mature opéra comique

Rameau almost certainly had the better musical argument but the immediate future belonged to the followers of Rousseau. The heroic tragédies-lyriques lost popularity, while the sentimental pastoral pieces of opéra comique went from strength to strength. Soon a new generation of composers made opéra comique into a real musical force and a more flexible medium capable of encompassing different types of drama as well as comedy. Opéra-comique's greatest master of the 18th-century was the Belgian composer, André Grétry (1741–1813). His copious output of works included village love stories, oriental tales, and parodies. His greatest success however, was an early example of the long-lived 'rescue opera' which became popular around the end of the 18th and beginning of the 19th century: *Richard Coeur de Lion* (1784) told the romantic story of the minstrel Blondel, who secured the King's escape from captivity. Opéra comique survived the Revolutionary era and then was carried into the 19th century.

Gluck and opera reform

Meanwhile, in the second half of the 18th century, the prestige of French culture was equalling that of the Italians, and Rousseau's revolutionary views were having their repercussions outside France.

Opéra comique had quickly found its way to the courts of continental Europe and by the end of the 1750s in Vienna, court composer Christoph Willibald Gluck (1714–1787) was writing opéras comiques in the French style. Despite the challenge of the new light-hearted styles of French and Italian opera though, serious opera still had a strong foothold in Vienna, even if, from time to time, the desirability of a more dramatic and less ornate form of opera had been argued.

Such a reform was finally accomplished by Gluck. In an atmosphere already primed for change, Gluck composed his first reform opera, *Orfeo ed Euridice* in 1762, in collaboration with librettist Rainieri Calzabigi, newly arrived from Paris. In his outlook on opera, Gluck was rather a curious mixture: He was obviously influenced by the new developments in France and in many ways he spoke the language of Rousseau, declaring that he believed music should be capable of 'imitation of nature' and of 'moving the heart and exciting the affection'. But on the whole, his works belonged to the tradition of French tragédie-lyrique.

Gluck's reforms created opera that was more credible. His music has none of the richness and complexity of Rameau's but it is utterly faithful to the situations on stage. In his operas, plot was simplified and dance and spectacle were made subordinate to the musical content, or eliminated altogether. The orchestra and chorus for the first time became as important as the soloists, and after *Orfeo*, he dispensed with the beautiful but artificial singing of castrati.

Gluck is the earliest composer to be included in the standard repertory today and is, without doubt, one of the great figures of operatic history. His operas mark the beginning of a trend for the deeper integration of drama with music and, in many ways, Romantic opera in the 19th century was built upon the foundations he had laid.

Despite pressure to close, Vaudeville plays became popular at the Foire de Saint-Germain in 1715, and by the end of the 18th century, the term opéra comique had come to mean any type of French opera containing spoken dialogue. But the essence of the early opéras comiques, which were brought to perfection by composers such as Grétry, Monsigny and Philidor, was preserved in the 19th-century in the form of popular musical comedy – operetta (pages 53-6).

Chapter 6

Singspiel

Singspiel, with its down-to-earth appeal and lively tunes, helped break Italian domination of opera in 18th-century Germany and led to the formation of a unique national style.

As Italian opera flowed out of 17th-century Italy across Europe, it made a great impression in the south German states. It was welcomed particularly by the nobility, many of whom were prepared to pay enormous salaries to exponents of the new style. The northern states, however, did not accept the Italian style so readily and the 18th century saw a continuing struggle between the strong taste for Italian-style opera in the southern provinces, including Vienna, and the emergence of the uniquely German style – *Singspiel* – in the north. Although Italian opera never really lost its foothold until the 19th century, Singspiel eventually conquered the

elite tastes of Vienna, and with its colour, spontaneity and appeal to the masses, it was on a par with opera buffa in Italy, and opéra-comique in France. With Mozart's *Die Zauberflöte (The Magic Flute)* as its supreme example, Singspiel laid the foundations for the establishment of a strong and individual German national style of opera.

Before the Italian onslaught, native German music drama had been pretty turgid affairs. Usually based on religious subjects, they were written mainly by the local clergy. These pious, moral plays which had been common in the 16th and early 17th century, were the roots of an early German national style.

Visiting troupes of Italian Commedia dell'arte players (below) during the 18th century were an important influence on the development of Germany's first national style of opera – Singspiel. This type of opera became popular among ordinary people in Vienna and equalled the Italian opera buffa.

Resistance to Italian opera

When opera arrived in Germany in the 17th century great rivalry developed between contemporary German monarchs and princelings who sought to better each other in the splendour of their new found Italian music. It was not long before German composers such as Hasse, Graun and Handel began to ape the Italian style and traditional German music fell far behind the new genre.

In northern Germany, however, native composers and performers resented the imposition of Italian culture and, on a more practical level, coveted the enormous fees the Italian performers commanded. One such individual, Nikolaus Strungk, was one of the first to champion the idea of a German national School. He built an opera house in Leipzig in 1689 and boldly attempted to direct Italian operas translated into the German language. Such translation was (and remains) extremely difficult, especially with the difference in diction between heavily stressed German compared to the relatively

'Hanswurst' (left) was the most popular of the early German Singspiel players, who amused (and shocked) audiences with his smutty humour. He appears even in Mozart's Magic Flute, *in an evolved form, as the wine- and women-loving Papageno.*

unstressed Italian language. Put simply, the words did not fit the music. Despite his efforts Strungk was not successful and he died leaving huge debts.

Audiences in Leipzig and Hamburg, however, were reluctant to welcome Catholic opera which was becoming more and more popular in the cities of southern Germany and Austria. An important rift developed between the Protestant north and Catholic south of Germany. The divide also grew along social lines, with national style being preferred by ordinary people.

This fight for national opera in Germany was joined by the composers Mattheson and Tellemann, but eventually even the northern city of Hamburg succumbed to Italian style. Its victory was foreshadowed by the *Hamburg period* opera of Handel, who began writing many of his arias in Italian. By around the 1740s, Italian opera had gained a foothold all over Germany, but just as Italian serious opera was reaching its peak in Europe, things were already gradually starting to change.

By the middle of the 18th century, the centre of opera had moved from Venice to Naples, whose rich musical culture was developed by its famous conservatoires and by the encouragement of the Neapolitan court. But opera seria – which had reached its height there – did not suit the palate of northern Germany, and considerable opposition to Italy's influence sprang up again.

The difference between the German and Italian styles of opera is reflected in the stark facade of Hamburg's second opera house, built in 1763 (far left), and the florid Italian stage set (left) of the same period.

The German response

The German answer to Italian opera seria appeared in 1773 with *Alceste,* the first wholly German five-act opera. The composer Anton Schweitzer (1753–87) teamed up with the great German poet, Christoph Martin Weiland, to produce a work sung in German from start to finish, striking an important blow for 'great' German opera. In marked contrast to the Italians, there were no castrato roles and coloratura singing – florid pieces for soprano – were avoided. The style of *Alceste* demonstrated a genuinely Germanic spirit to which the romantic opera of the 19th century can be traced.

Singspiel – opera for the people

Meanwhile, German composers had also begun to develop their own equivalent of comic opera already emerging elsewhere in Europe. And it was this new style which was finally to give Germany an operatic identity to equal Italy and France. German audiences had never been keen on the Italian tendency to avoid spoken dialogue in opera. They preferred to reserve the use of music for the high spots of the drama, and rely on spoken dialogue to keep the story moving. The fact that ordinary people increasingly rejected what they saw as a courtly art, which was totally foreign to them both in language and expression, contributed to the rise of a new form of native German opera – *Singspiel.*

'Singspiel' means literally, 'singing play', and it continued the traditions laid down by generations of vagrant actors and musicians who, centuries before, had performed religious plays in medieval times. Their refreshing performances also owed much to German folk music and were clearly inspired by similar operatic movements in France and Britain. The popular guise of Singspiel took beggars, thieves and prostitutes as its heroes, while its music often mocked what was seen as the pretentious warbling of Italian music and the snobbishness of the nobility's taste.

As these ballad operas became more and more popular, the Prussian Ambassador to London, von Brock, translated Charles Coffey's *The Devil to Pay* which, first performed in Berlin in 1743 as *Der Teufel ist Los,* was hugely successful. And with this work, the Singspiel era began in earnest.

Another successful English import was an imitation of *The Beggar's Opera,* by J. C. Pepusch and John Gay, and performed at Covent Garden in 1728. J. A. Hiller adapted the opera for German audiences, and its enormous box office success gave Hiller the title of 'Father of Singspiel'. German audiences soon warmed to these farces full of catchy tunes and simple melodies that they could remember long after the performance, rather than just a display of vocal acrobatics from Italian sopranos.

At first, Hiller centred his productions at Leipzig, but the popular Singspiel style soon arrived in Vienna – the southern bastion of Italian opera. Here, the style of Singspiel borrowed heavily from Italian opera buffa and became, overall, a more varied and sophisticated genre – with comedy that incorporated some Italian-style arias as well. The more refined Viennese audiences were generally condescending about the tastes of the Protestant north of Germany, and remained more loyal to Italian-style drama and poetry.

Even if the wealthier classes scorned popular opera, the ordinary people of Vienna enjoyed it immensely and welcomed wandering performers who brought Singspiel to the city. One Singspiel character, in particular, went down well with the audiences. He was Hanswurst, the narrator. The

For a time, Singspiel became the dominant style of opera, under the patronage of Emperor Joseph II (above).

narrator took the part of the cosmopolitan jester or harlequin and he and the other narrators delighted the audience with a barrage of risqué, smutty jokes throughout the performances. Many connoisseurs of more refined opera deplored what they saw as the vulgarity of popular Singspiel. One correspondent of *Berlinische Musikalische Zeitung* expressed utter disbelief that the public should applaud 'this miserable fellow (Hanswurst), who is not entirely without some comic ability, but whose utterances would offend any decent person'.

Singspiel in Vienna

Seeing all this going on in his capital city, the enlightened Austrian Emperor, Joseph II, viewed Singspiel as a means of advancing a uniquely German musical culture. He realized that Singspiel could become, to German speaking Europe, what opera buffa was to Italy. Joseph, therefore, ordered the establishment of a national Singspiel theatre in Vienna, which was opened on 16 January, 1778. The success of its opening encouraged Joseph to commission Mozart, who up until then had been concentrating on composing in the Italian style, to produce his famous *Die Entführung aus dem Serail* (The Abduction from the Seraglio – 1782). This is regarded by many as the definitive Singspiel – sunny, sentimental and filled with wonderful light music.

For a time, the national Singspiel of Joseph II even threatened the existence of Italian opera in Vienna. Whereas the Protestant north called for the participation of amateur actors and singers, the Viennese, as always, demanded the best singers, the best orchestras and the finest church choristers to perform their Singspiels. The lead given by Dittersdorf and Mozart was followed by the works of Wenzel Muller and Joseph Weigl and turned Vienna, at the end of the 18th century, into a unique musical metropolis.

By the beginning of the 1790s, Mozart's operas held audiences and musicians spellbound. In particular, *The Magic Flute* (1791) received the ultimate accolade of being translated into Italian. With this piece, Mozart proved his genius by fusing together Singspiel-type popular music and serious music to produce a masterly work.

Strangely, the seemingly sound foothold gained by Singspiel did not remain firm. Joseph II was as much a dabbler in music as he was in politics and diplomacy. His national Singspiel was short-lived, closing in 1798, only 10 years after its opening. He wanted a German national opera for political reasons, but his own preference and that of the Italian court remained for Italian-style grand opera. When the Italian composer Antonio Salieri won Joseph's favour, he encouraged in the Emperor, the view that Singspiel was pretty thin stuff. More importantly, significant developments were taking place in politics and society, which were having a profound effect on the late 18th-century world, leaving less of a place for light-hearted Singspiel. The French Revolution and the ensuing Napoleonic wars destroyed the stability of much of Europe, while industrialization and urbanization changed social values. The invading revolutionary armies of Napoleon meant that Europe had become pre-occupied with more serious issues.

By 1795, a new generation of composers began to emerge to reflect these new realities. Haydn had composed his last great symphony and Mozart was already four years in his grave. But the contribution made by Viennese Singspiel and its challenge to Italian opera had prepared the way for Germany's future musical greatness during the 19th century. It had finally given Germany a true national identity in the operatic world from which she was to leap forward as the leader of operatic style in the Romantic age.

Mozart's great comic opera of 1782, **The Abduction from the Seraglio** *(right) was one of the most successful works to be written for Emperor Joseph II's national Singspiel theatre. Along with* **The Magic Flute,** *this is Singspiel in its finest form.*

Chapter 7

Revolution in France

The Great Revolution broke many old traditions in France – not least the Classical style of opera. And for the following 100 years the story of opera was one of continual change.

The course of opera in France between the end of the 18th century and the beginning of the 19th is a tortuous one. Triggered by the Great Revolution of 1789, opera suddenly moved away from the established Classical style and set off in a completely new direction. But this was not to last, and the following years were to see elements of earlier traditions reassert themselves, before the dying years of the 19th century brought further change.

'Revolutionary' opera

No aspect of European life was left entirely untouched by the cataclysmic effects of the French Revolution of 1789. In France itself the effects on the course of opera were immediate and profound. At first opera was a target for attack – it was, after all, characteristically the very symbol and preserve of aristocratic privilege, as it had been throughout its past. Indeed, the whole institution, embodied by the Opéra, fell under royal patronage and this made it even more unpalatable to the rising masses. Consequently, when Paris rose in 1789 the Opéra was closed down altogether. But as the Revolution got under way operatic composers became caught up in the social and political idealism of the times and realized that opera could be used to promote and reflect the revolutionary cause. Thus the Opéra was reopened under the control of the City of Paris and staged works 'for the people' – works with Revolutionary themes, such as *The Triumph of the Republic* and *The Chance of Liberty*.

New laws passed during this period also allowed anyone to open a theatre and to stage operas: previously all theatres were licensed and controlled by the state and were relatively few and far between. The common theme of nearly all the new operas was their political message, carried along by an exciting story. Thrills were the order of the day, both in the writing and the staging. Melodrama was in; traditional classical pomposity and splendour were out – except where they served a political purpose.

The result of this experimentation led to the emergence of the 'rescue opera' which became the rage of Paris during the 1790s. Stories varied from horror tales about robbers and tyrants to romantic tales of chivalry, but they all had one thing in common – the rescue of the hero or heroine at the eleventh hour, by brave deeds or supreme sacrifices.

The Emperor Napoleon (right) used the Paris Opéra as a stage to glorify his own majesty and that of his empire. In doing so he helped set French opera on the road to Grand Opera – a style that was to be important through the 19th century.

Among the new smaller theatres, two in particular rose to prominence, the Favart and the Feydeau. A fierce rivalry existed and each theatre had its own clique of composers. Competition between them finally ceased when they merged in 1801 under the name of the Opéra-Comique.

Meanwhile, over at the Opéra, the sense of adventure sparked by the Revolution was beginning to fade. And as Napoleon took a grip on all France so he turned to establishing personal control of the Opéra. By 1802 he had personal veto over everything the Opéra staged and had returned it to its former position as the leading operatic institution. Then, in 1811, he delivered the little theatres of Paris a crushing blow by making them pay dues to the Opéra. Many went out of business, leaving only the Opéra-Comique and the recently established Théâtre Italien as major alternative venues to the Opéra.

The first Grand Operas

The most spectacular product of Napoleon's grandiose ideas for the Opéra was Spontini's *Fernando Cortez,* staged there in 1809. The idea for the opera came from the Emperor himself – it was supposed to vindicate his campaign in Spain – and no expense was spared in staging. It outdid even the pre-Revolutionary operas in scale and magnificence – one of the highlights was a full-scale cavalry charge. But most Parisians found the lighter works staged at the Opéra-Comique and the run of Italian operas at the Théâtre Italien – notably Rossini's *Barber of Seville* – much more to their taste and continued to do so for another decade. Then, with a glittering production of *Aladdin* by Isouard in 1822, the Opéra began to turn heads once more.

For *Aladdin* gas lighting was used for the first time in opera, and this in combination with the wonderful backdrops painted by Jacques Daguerre – who later invented the first practical photographic process – produced breathtakingly real scenery. Daguerre was a brilliant illusionist painter who made his name with *dioramas* which were all the rage in Paris and

French Grand Opera in the 19th century owes much to German composer Giacomo Meyerbeer (above left). His famous Robert the Devil *(1831) enraptured French audiences devoted to spectacle. The above scene shows the celebrated tenor, Adolphe Nourrit, (for whom the title role was originally created) in melodramatic pose, torn between the forces of good and evil. Melodramatic heroism was an essential ingredient of French Grand Opera and equally so were the spectacular visual effects. The set designs for Meyerbeer's* Les Huguenots *(far right) and Halevy's* La Juive *(right) are typical of the style in their scale and grandeur.*

London at the time. Dioramas, like modern-day planetariums, used all kinds of optical tricks to bring painted scenes to life, and Daguerre, along with the Opéra's principal designer deployed these tricks on the Opéra's stage to marvellous effect – many people went along simply for the spectacle. Daguerre's greatest triumph, perhaps, was the staging of the eruption of the volcano Vesuvius at the end of Auber's *La Muette de Portici* (The dumb girl of Portici) (1828), climaxing with a huge shower of stones on the stage as the curtain fell.

La Muette was a triumph in more ways than one, for it finally put the Opéra back in the vanguard of French opera and established the 'Grand' style that was lapped up by the Parisians for the next 30 years. It was the fulfilment of the revolution fomented by Rossini after he became director of the Theatre-Italien in 1824. Rossini combined the melody and power of Italian opera with the French sense of theatre and historical realism. In *La Muette* the combination was so sensational that Rossini himself was inspired to write a Grand Opera, *William Tell* (1829), perhaps the greatest of all Grand Operas.

La Muette also marked the arrival of Eugene Scribe as a librettist. Scribe is often dismissed as a hack playwright, and his work is undeniably 'commercial' – he regularly wrote ten plays a month, ten months a year. But as a librettist, he held first place on the Parisian scene for over 30 years. What Scribe did was take historical-romantic dramas made popular by writers like Victor Hugo and combine this with the illusionist spectacle already successful at the Opéra. The combination was a sure-fire hit with Parisian audiences, and ensured Grand Opera's continued domination of serious opera in Paris throughout the

1830s and 40s. Scribe was not one to drop a successful formula, and he and the German composer Meyerbeer, collaborated on a string of hits such as *Robert le Diable* (1831) and *Les Huguenots* (1836).

With Daniel Auber, Scribe found an equally successful formula, this time for light opera, and the pair exploited it mercilessly. They wrote 28 operas together for the Opéra-Comique, nearly all of them hugely popular and nearly all of them instantly forgettable. They relied on a well-crafted plot and a range of amusing titillating situations, such as the heroine's undressing in *Fra Diavolo*. Auber set this off with lively, bouncing music that never drops below *andante* in pace. He was still scoring hits at the age of 86 (in 1868).

Eventually, however, Parisian audiences and musicians began to tire of the kind of superficial excitement provided on the one hand by the Opéra, with its hollow and grandiose spectacle, and by the Opéra-Comique with its 'pop' operas on the other. One new direction was the frivolous, exuberant satires of Offenbach which soon became enormously popular. Another was the attempt, led by Leon Carvalho at the Théâtre Lyrique (founded in 1847), to foster a more worthy form of light opera.

New life for opéra comique

For many years then, opéra comique had been languishing in the lap of commercialism, with composers like Auber never short of successes, so long as they stuck to the formula. All this time, no new spark appeared to lift the style out of its stagnant state. It was not until shortly after the mid-century that the Théâtre Lyrique finally saw the premières of some of the most important opéras comiques of the

Motley Books Ltd.

34

After the great commercial successes of Grand Opera in mid-century, the operatic tide in France then turned towards a more natural style of expression. Offenbach's Contes d'Hoffmann *(set design right) was first performed at the Opéra-Comique in 1881. Although concerned with the supernatural it introduced characters that were realistic and believable.*

century – namely Gounod's *Faust* (1859) and *Mireille* (1864), and Bizet's *Pearl Fishers* (1863) and *The Fair Maid of Perth* (1867).

These operas were strongly Romantic, being termed 'comique' because they followed the earlier tradition of Rousseau, in that they appealed to the heart rather than the eye, and their characters were warm and human. Also, the classification of operas as 'comique' or otherwise, often came down to whether they contained spoken dialogue or not. So even operas that dealt with obviously serious themes came to be called, if somewhat confusingly, 'comique'.

With the decline of the Théâtre Lyrique from 1870, the younger French composers turned back to the Opéra-Comique, now directed by the imaginative Camille du Locle. In the early 1870s, early works by Massenet, Saint-Saëns and Delibes were put on there. So too were Berlioz's *Trojans at Carthage* and further works by Bizet. Few of Bizet's works were particularly successful, until, in 1875, the year Bizet died, the Opéra-Comique mounted a production of his last opera, *Carmen*. This opera, Bizet's greatest achievement, and the finest of all opéras comiques, paradoxically, sounded the death knell for this style. The regular audience at the Opéra-Comique were shocked by the savagery and sensuality of the work. But the realism and violent emotion were difficult to forget, and *Carmen* inspired a long string of *verismo* (true-to-life) operas, notably by Italian composers such as Mascagni, Leoncavallo and Puccini.

Carmen also blurred the distinction between the Opéra-Comique's and the Opéra's style, for Bizet's opera was as serious in its tragedy as anything put on at the Opéra. The works of Jules Massenet, the leading French opera composer of the 1880s and 90s, were as likely to be premiered at the Opéra as at the Opéra-Comique, even though they were essentially lyrical romantic tales.

With the breakdown of the barrier between serious and light opera, French opera began to pull in all kinds of directions, few ever having a lasting impact. Some French composers such as Charpentier tried the realistic style. Others tried to follow influences from abroad, notably Wagner's powerful romantic style. Many young French composers made the pilgrimage to Bayreuth, where the 'music dramas' were making a huge impact in the world of opera.

THE CLAQUE

In France during the 19th century the phenomenon of the *Claque* came into its own. The word 'claque' comes from the French for 'smack' or 'clap', and in opera refers to a group of people specially hired either to applaud or to shout down a particular performance, in order to help ensure its success or to guarantee its failure. Although claques had existed before, in 18th-century Italian opera houses for example, 19th-century France saw its real systematic use. In Paris, in 1820, there was even a Claque agency.

The Claque was no ramshackle mob of screaming banshees, it was usually a sophisticated, well organized affair. The team of *Claqueurs* was carefully divided into specialist noise-makers who were orchestrated by the leader – *le chef de claque*. From a good vantage point in the auditorium he would direct his team: there were *tapageurs,* who led with extra loud applause; *connaisseurs,* who made vociferous knowledgeable remarks; *pleureurs,* who made great play of squeezing out copious tears of emotion; *bisseurs,* who called repeatedly for encores – and *chauffeurs,* who spread the word, good or bad, before, during and after performances.

Claqueurs were usually in the pay of someone with a vested interest in the success or failure of the show and such was their effectiveness, particularly when reacting unfavourably, that many a now-great opera was seen to fail during its early run.

Chapter 8

Weber and Wagner

The Romantic period in Germany produced two outstanding composers – Carl Maria von Weber and Richard Wagner. Together they helped thrust Germany to the forefront of 19th-century opera.

Romanticism – the great intellectual and artistic movement which spanned the 19th century – made its mark in all the arts, not least opera, shortly after the French Revolution. In Germany two figures dominated the Romantic movement: Carl Maria von Weber, who was instrumental in forging it; and Richard Wagner, who took the movement to new heights. After the regionalism that had divided Germany in the 18th century – with the Protestant north and Catholic south adopting different styles of Singspiel – the works of these two composers finally brought unity. And from the shadow of French Grand Opera they created a strong national style, pushing Germany to the lead in the operatic world.

One of the first signs of the birth of the new style was the inheritance, from France, of the 'rescue'

opera. Heroic drama and last-minute escape from the jaws of doom were the essence of these often highly political works. Even mighty Beethoven was inspired by the genre to write his only opera – *Fidelio* (1805). This, though, was really part Singspiel, part rescue opera, and it was no great success at first, even though it contains some powerful music. *Fidelio* thus proved to be only the herald of the age of German Romantic opera. This really began around 1820.

'The Free Shot'
In 1817 the young Carl Weber (1786–1826) asked the poet Friedrich Kind to write him a libretto. Shortly afterwards, in a letter to his wife, his excitement suggests that he already had an inkling of the great stir that *Der Freischütz* would produce.

In 1820, Weber's **The Marksman** *appeared (the final dramatic scene from which is shown below) and launched German opera into its exciting Romantic phase. Legend, the occult and the supernatural became characterisitc themes.*

The Marksman made Carl Maria von Weber (above, 1786–1826) the most famous composer in Germany. His works had a far-reaching influence on German Romantic music – including Wagner's operas later in the century.

Friedrich Kind is going to begin an opera book for me. The subject is admirable, interesting and horribly exciting . . . there's the very devil in it. He appears as the Black Huntsman; the bullets are made in a ravine at midnight, with special apparitions around. Haven't I made your flesh creep on your bones?

Der Freischütz, literally translated, means 'The Free Shot'. It is the story of a marksman who, in order to win a contest, buys seven magic bullets from the Devil. Six, he is assured, will hit the bullseye but the seventh, as part of the bargain, is reserved for the Devil himself – for a 'free shot'.

A preoccupation with the supernatural, history, legends and fairytales was one of the most important features of Romantic opera, and in Germany, where literature at the time was full of supernatural happenings and beings (Faust, for example), an interest in the occult and the magical distinguished it from the Romantic movements in France and Italy.

18th-century Singspiel had seen ordinary people rise to the fore as heroes of opera: now the humanized characters were, in some sense, portrayed as representatives of agents of supernatural forces, either good or evil. And the eventual victory, or demise, of the hero came to represent the abstract idea of the triumph of right over wrong. After the studied rationalism of the 18th century, the mysterious exotic forces of nature and the supernatural suddenly reawakened primitive emotions among cosily seated opera-goers and, in this, Weber hit the mark in every respect.

Only a few operas have given their composers instant stardom – *Der Freischütz* was one of them. The wild acclaim which greeted its première was a very fitting start to the new operatic era. The work opened at the new Schauspielhaus in Berlin in 1821, and the excited mood of the audience, which included many eminent artists of the day, was evident from the moment the overture was encored. The fierce applause that it received at the end confirmed it as a resounding success overall, and within the space of six months the opera had been presented to rapturous audiences throughout the whole of German-speaking Europe.

Wagner later called *Der Freischütz* the first German opera, but equally memorable was Weber's *Oberon* (1826), an English Singspiel, especially written for the Royal Opera House at Covent Garden. There is something of Shakespeare's *Midsummer Night's Dream* in this work, but in a Romantic, Oriental setting. After the opening night Weber wrote to his wife: 'Tonight I obtained the greatest success of my life.' It was a triumphant end to a tragically brief career. He had accepted the commission against doctor's orders, and just seven weeks later, still in London, Weber died of tuberculosis. He was eventually buried in Dresden – where he had been director of the German repertory of the theatre since 1817 – and in 1844 Richard Wagner gave a graveside oration in his honour.

After Weber's untimely demise there was, for a long time, no one to take up his mantle. Many German composers took up the challenge to write a Romantic opera but few took the formula to the hilt. In fact, in the years between 1830 and 1849 foreign opera, especially French, again dominated the German opera houses, and of the living composers, only Spohr, Lortzing, Kreutzer and Flowtow could match talent from abroad.

The genius of Wagner

The lull in German inspiration did not, however, persist. In fact, the best was yet to come. In 1843 the first performance of a wonderful operatic ghost story, *The Flying Dutchman,* marked the arrival of a composer of genius – Richard Wagner. He became one of the most powerfully influential figures that opera has ever known.

Wagner made an enormous contribution to 19th-century culture. Singlehandedly he created an artistic revolution. His name is mentioned in the same breath as the other giants of the century – Marx, Freud and Darwin. Even the great philosopher Friedrich Nietzsche, one of the greatest thinkers of the century, fell under Wagner's spell – a tribute to Wagner's artistic and intellectual substance.

The Flying Dutchman, full of Weber-style music, was followed two years later by *Tannhäuser,* with similar success. But in 1849 Wagner was forced to flee his homeland to exile, after becoming involved in the political uprisings which shook the whole of Europe at the end of the 'hungry forties'. From his refuge on the shores of Lake Geneva, Wagner wrote his third great opera *Lohengrin* (1850), which was conducted at its first performance, in Wagner's absence, by Liszt. In these three operas, he embraced the lands of myth and legend and through them called for a return of the heroic spirit of the past.

Apart from his immense musical talent Wagner also had great literary ability. For his time, he was unique in writing the libretti for all his operas. But living for so many years away from close contact with German theatre, Wagner became obsessed with

Wagner set the pattern for the German Romantic Opera movement and sought to recapture the spirit of the past with elaborate, realistic sets and authentic costumes. He wrote Parsifal (1882, above), a story of the Knights of the Holy Grail, specifically for his own opera house at Bayreuth. The original Bayreuth theatre (right) was far too antiquated to produce the powerful and integrated effects that Wagner conceived for his operas.

Lauros-Giraudon

the grandeur of his own ideas. It was during this time that he began work on his great four-part work *The Ring*. He had set out to write just one drama, *Siegfried's Death*, a story from an ancient legendary epic, about the decline and fall of the Norse gods — the *Nibelungenlied*. But the story was so involved that Wagner ended up writing the four operas of *The Ring*. The work was the culmination of Wagner's Romanticism. Indeed the project became so large in its conception and scale that Wagner realized he would need a new theatre to present the work.

The Festival Theatre at Bayreuth

Wagner's dream became a practical possibility when he came under the protection of Ludwig II of Bavaria. The young king, captivated by Wagner's master-piece, *Tristan and Isolde* (1865) became a great admirer of Wagner's music. Royal patronage made the idea of a Festival Theatre a reality.

It was built at Bayreuth, not far from Nürnberg, and opened in 1876 with the first complete performance of *The Ring*. The theatre was one of the finest in Europe and its whole conception was devoted to maximizing the impact and the enjoyment of opera. The fan-shaped auditorium gave each seat in the house an equally good view of the stage. But more importantly, the orchestra was housed in a specially built pit, beneath the stage, to conceal it from the view of both singers and audience.

The spirit and style of Bayreuth spread all over the world. Applause and encores during the course of a performance were banished because they would have spoiled the continuity of Wagnerian opera. For the same reason latecomers were not permitted to enter until an intermission. Similarly, lights were dimmed during the performance — the audience had to be completely immersed in the power and emotion of the piece.

There is no doubt that Wagner's work had a profound effect on all subsequent opera. In his music, he left the formalized aria/recitative structure far behind. His operas were characterized by flowing continuity, with a lattice of leading motifs (leitmotiven) which take the listener through a web of subtle implications of character and emotion. His dramas presented a total fusion of the arts — a communion of poetry, décor, lighting and staging, all conceived and masterminded by Wagner himself.

Wagner's particular use of symbolism and mythology though, were difficult to imitate, and although his innovations actually changed the face of opera forever, no composer could continue in the unique vein he had created. German Romantic opera, then, impressed itself on late 19th-century Europe through its sheer overwhelming power to create an all-embracing state of emotion. Throughout Europe the mood of Romanticism was closely linked with strong feelings of nationalism, and the spirit of Wagnerian opera did much to fan the flames of German national consciousness. The power and influence of Wagner in the operatic world could only be matched by one other composer in Europe: Giuseppe Verdi became as great a national institution in Italy as Wagner did in Germany. In Verdi's hands Italian Romantic opera dealt with very different subject matter, but the music was as powerfully stirring.

In September 1882 Wagner — who was by now suffering a serious heart condition — and his family travelled to Venice. A year later a final heart attack ended his life. He was buried in the garden of Wahnfried at Bayreuth.

Heinrich 'Scene from Parsifal'/Giancarlo Costa

Gustav Bauernfeind 'Interior of Margrave's Opera House, Bayreuth'. Munich Theatre Museum. Joachim Blauel/Artothek

Chapter 9

Opera's Golden Age

19th-century Italian composers embraced the spirit of Romanticism with a passion which inspired some of the most powerful operas of all time – many of which have become firm favourites.

Giancarlo Costa

As the mood of Romanticism swept across Europe in the early 19th century, it sparked off in Italy, as it had in France and Germany, a radically new operatic style. Italian Romantic composers left behind the stiff and rigid traditions of opera seria and turned instead to writing historical dramas full of high passion and set in wild and barbarous landscapes. Displays of unrestrained emotions from the characters gave new scope for virtuoso singing, and the cult of the star singer – particularly the prima donna – became the rage of the age. And with the dawning of Italian Romanticism opera entered its 'Golden Age.'

Italian Romanticism

Romanticism began to make inroads into Italian art generally, after the end of the Napoleonic Wars, in 1815. At the time the leading Italian composer was Gioacchino Rossini (1792–1868). Rossini never embraced Romanticism – he was essentially a traditionalist composing in the classical style. But he continued to find success in a world that was changing around him and no doubt this was due to

the irresistible verve, tunefulness and wit of his music, as shown in such works as his enduringly popular *Barber of Seville*.

However, even in Rossini, there were signs of a new approach. His *Otello* (1816) was inspired by Shakespeare, and Shakespeare was to become a favourite source of the Romantics. Rossini also composed for libretti which were based on works by Sir Walter Scott, notably *The Lady of the Lake* (1819) and *Ivanhoe* (1826). The historical novels of Scott, with their medieval and northern settings, enjoyed huge popularity in 19th-century Europe. With their dramatic plots and Romantic backdrops, they inspired dozens of Italian Romantic operas.

Rossini retired – inexplicably – at the age of 37 while still apparently at the height of his powers. The two composers then to take the lead in Italian opera were Gaetano Donizetti (1797–1848) and Vincenzo Bellini (1801–35) and they were the first to take the plunge into writing full-blooded Romantic opera. Romanticism in opera had the same preoccupations as it did in the other arts – the ideals of the Age of

A sacred forest in ancient Gaul (above) was the setting for part of Bellini's Romantic opera Norma *(1830). Scenes of nature remote and untamed were a typical feature of Italian opera in the first half of the 19th century, often reflecting the natural passions of the characters.*

Enlightenment were thrown aside and it was the emotions that ruled over order, and instinct over reason. Self-expression became all important and the freedom of the spirit was often reflected in natural and wild settings.

All these things were the essence of Donizetti's and Bellini's Romantic operas, which were full of fiery passions and took place in exotic lands or times. Bellini's *Norma* (1831) is set in ancient Gaul and tells the story of the guilty passion of a Druid priestess for a Roman officer. Donizetti's *Lucia di Lammermoor* (1835) and Bellini's *The Puritans* (1835), both based on novels by Scott, were set in the wilds of the Scottish highlands. In addition, *Lucia* includes the famous 'Mad Scene' in which the heroine is driven to the very limits of distress – a typical symptom of Romantic preoccupation with extremes – and very soon every tragic opera had to include its own token mad scene!

Donizetti and Bellini also continued Rossini's practice of writing for the voices of specific performers. In fact, the strong personality and dynamic acting ability of one of the most famous of the 19th-century prima donnas, Giuditta Pasta, actually inspired the title role of Bellini's *Norma*.

By this time, *bel canto* (literally 'beautiful singing') had entered a new golden age (see p. 40)

and the two composers filled their works with wonderful arias, especially designed to show off the vocal powers of their celebrity singers. These pieces were less formal in pattern than their 18th-century equivalents and the highly ornamented arias gave vent to a stream of violent emotion. When combined with impassioned acting by stars such as Pasta, Maria Malibran, Giulia and Giuditta Grisi, who seemed to live out their parts on stage, audiences glimpsed the very depths of human tragedy.

Bellini died, only 34, leaving a legacy of far fewer operas than his contemporary, Donizetti. As a slower

Historical dramas were the favourite subjects of the Italian Romantics and the scenes from Ivanhoe, Edward in Scotland *and* Norma *(left, above and top right) feature some of the most famous 19th-century singers. Shown right is the Swedish soprano Jenny Lind in the 'mad scene' from* Lucia di Lammermoor.

Giancarlo Costa

Kungl. Husgeradskammaren, Stockholm

worker and a perfectionist Bellini's operas were of much more constant quality than Donizetti's and they contain some of the most exquisitely beautiful melodies that opera has known. Donizetti, on the other hand, was prolific. In his lifetime he wrote over 70 operas, but it is sometimes said of him that he produced too much too quickly. Unlike Bellini, Donizetti wrote both comic and tragic opera and some of his finest achievements were actually comedies. With him opera buffa was kept alive just a little longer and his *Love Potion* (1832), *The Daughter of the Regiment* (1840) and *Don Pasquale* (1843) were outstanding examples. Comedy though, was going out of fashion (perhaps because it seemed too frivolous to a generation preoccupied with Romantic-nationalist feeling) and after *Don Pasquale,* no important comic opera was composed in Italy for 50 years and serious subjects were the basis of most 19th century operas.

As well as its fascination for the drama of individuals, the Romantic spirit also embraced a whole new popular idealism that was sweeping Europe. The huge social upheavals that were going on sparked off an intellectual revolution amongst all artists and the most rousing events of the day became another source for their inspiration. The Romantics thrilled to the stirrings of the democratic revolution in Europe where, instead of the mob they saw 'people' rising towards a new world full of hope.

Viva Verdi!

Amidst all this was the popular cause for political unity in Italy and it is not surprising that the heroic energy and dramatic intensity of Verdi's music came to encapsulate the hopes of the Italian people.

Verdi wrote 27 operas during his lifetime, his art developing slowly and steadily over several decades. Three of his best-loved masterpieces appeared in the early·1850s – *Rigoletto* (1851), *Il Trovatore* (1853) and *La Traviata* (1853) and through these Verdi had already begun to make major steps forward in the development of operatic form. He began to eliminate the display arias of his predecessors and to contrive arias and ensembles that expressed character and the dramatic situation more naturally. In his hands too, the orchestra was used to the full and the overall result was a form of music-drama at once unified, subtle and utterly compelling. Verdi's advances culminated in the masterpieces of his old age, *Otello* (1887) and *Falstaff* (1893).

Verismo

Towards the end of the century, there was a new move among some composers to introduce more realistic subjects or 'a slice of life' into opera. The movement, known as *verismo,* was inspired by Bizet's *Carmen* (1875) in that it focused on the lives of common people instead of aristocrats, and tackled low-life, even seedy, situations. In Italy the first verismo successes were Mascagni's *Cavalleria Rusticana* (1890) and Leoncavallo's *I Pagliacci* (1892) but it was Giacomo Puccini (1858–1924) who became the style's greatest exponent. With such masterpieces as *La Bohème* (1896) and *Madam Butterfly* (1904), his operas were filled with realistic local colour.

So it was that Puccini took opera into the 20th century where, once again, old values and old forms were cast aside in a quest for the modern and the new. In the new century opera was soon to see some of the most revolutionary, and at times bizarre, productions of all time.

BEL CANTO

In mid 19th century Italy, the long-lived fashion for particularly florid singing, known as 'bel canto', finally came to an end. The style reached its first peak between 1720 and 1790 in the age of the castrati, when the display arias and set-piece duets of opera seria were the order of the day. Then, in the early 19th century, Rossini advocated a return to Italy's national singing style and his example was followed by Romantic composers Donizetti and Bellini.

In the 18th century, virtuoso singing was greatly admired by audiences – often to the annoyance of composers whose music would be at the mercy of egotistical performers who loved to embellish their roles. Rossini, on the other hand, wrote with the voices of specific singers in mind, and managed to pre-empt any gratuitous ornamentation by writing an already florid vocal line into his scores. For Bellini and Donizetti, the intense emotions of Romantic opera found ideal expression through such displays of vocal virtuosity. Their famous 'mad scenes', where the soprano went into an apparently deranged state, demanded some of the most precise and highly skilled vocal acrobatics from their singers.

Verdi opted mainly for a more dramatically credible singing style and bel canto subsequently went into decline. In the 1950s however, Maria Callas revived many of the old and forgotten 19th-century bel canto roles and brought the style renewed popularity with audiences. Today Joan Sutherland continues to be as associated with the title role of Donizetti's *Lucia di Lammermoor,* the most famous bel canto opera to survive in the modern repertory.

Giancarlo Costa

The greatest singer of the 19th-century bel canto *era was Italian soprano Giuditta Pasta. Shown left in the title role of Donizetti's* Ann Boleyn *(1830), her legendary interpretations and poignant singing inspired a string of roles by Romantic composers.*

Chapter 10

Russian Opera

With its themes of history and heroism, folklore and fantasy, Russian opera suddenly cut loose from its European ties in the 19th century and blossomed into a striking and original art.

Opera came to Russia from Italy in the first half of the 18th century but it was not until the next century that Russia began to forge its own national style. In the 19th century Russian opera flowered as composers, spurred on by fervent nationalism, began to draw on their own country's history as well as a rich tradition of folk-song melody, to create works of intense musical colour and great patriotic pride.

At the start, opera in Russia was exclusively dominated by the West. Ever since the reign of Peter the Great (1672–1725), when the imperial court had moved to St Petersburg, Russia had opened its gateway to European influence. Under the Empress Anna Ivanova, Peter's niece, plays, balls, and all kinds of musical entertainments were the favourite courtly pastimes of the day.

The Empress encouraged many foreign artists to bring their talents to her court and by the 1720s, Italian singers began to travel to Russia to perform. It was not long before the first Italian opera was staged there – a comic intermezzo, *Calandro,* by a composer named Ristori, was given in 1731.

In 1735, the Empress Anna chose a Neapolitan composer, Francesco Araia, to be her *Maestro di capella.* Araia's *La Forza dell 'Amore* was performed the next year, and more Italian operas followed.

After Anna Ivanova, the Empress Catherine the Great (1729–1796) became one of opera's most important patrons. Priding herself as one of the world's enlightened monarchs, she invited a string of

A performance of Mussorgsky's Boris Godunov by the Bolshoi Company, Moscow (above). This classic opera is Russia's best known work. Its patriotic theme is typical of other operas of the 19th-century Nationalist school in that it celebrates an heroic figure from Russian history.

The 1836 set design for Ivan Susanin and Ruslan and Lyudmila by Mikhail Ivanovich Glinka (1804-1857 above). These early Russian works show the influence of Glinka's four years in Italy, but in their phrasing and rhythm they echo native Russian folk music. Glinka, the father of Russian opera, drw inspiration from a wealth of native folk melodies to express all the shades of Russian life – its joys, its sadness and human struggles. Ivan Susanin and Ruslan and Lyudmila became models for Russian operas such as Mussorgsky's The Kovansky Rising *(1886).*

Italian composers, as well as other nationalities, to the court at St Petersburg. Among them were Galuppi, Tartini, Cimarosa and Paisiello (whose *Barber of Seville* (1782) was composed in Russia and initially was more popular in Italy than Rossini's later version).

Catherine also sent some of the best native musicians abroad to learn the coveted western techniques. When the first operas by Russian composers eventually appeared at the end of the 1870s, they were, understandably enough, simply Italian-style operas sung in Russian.

Such foreign domination proved extremely difficult to shake off. In the first hundred years of opera in Russia western themes remained the vogue, and any Russian attempts at opera continued to be composed in a distinct European mould.

It was not until the 1830s that, along with the great formative period of Russian music as a whole, Russian opera began to become a style of its own. The first Russian composer of outstanding talent was Mikhail Ivanovich Glinka (1804–1857) and he began Russia's long and fruitful journey from European dependence to new artistic freedom.

Glinka – the founder of the Nationalist school

As in 19th-century Europe, nationalism became an important artistic movement in Russia. The war of 1812 against the invading Napoleonic army, then the Crimean war in mid century, helped to unleash a creative outburst in which all the arts shone. Composers and writers began to delve into their own country's rich history for inspiration. One such was Glinka, the father of the great Nationalist school.

Like many other Russian composers, Glinka was a largely self-taught musician. Much of his musical knowledge had been gained while playing the violin in his uncle's serf orchestra. Four years in Italy, where he met both Bellini and Donizetti, and subsequent training in Berlin, gave Glinka both the burning desire and the tools to attempt to write opera. His *Ivan Susanin* (at one time called *A Life for the Tsar*) appeared in 1836 and shows Glinka's commitment to the creation of true Russian music. He said of the work: 'I could not become an Italian composer, and remembering my homeland with nostalgia, I gradually began to think of composing like a Russian.'

Both *Ivan Susanin* and his second opera, *Ruslan and Lyudmila* (1842), still show the influence of the Italian tradition of *bel canto,* but in their melodic phrasing and rhythm, the works are undeniably Russian, full of echoes of the native folk music that Glinka had heard in his youth. These two operas, with their heroic themes, and rousing choruses, became the model for a host of Russian operas.

A close friend of Glinka's, composer Alexander Dargomizhky (1813–1869), also made great strides for Russian opera in strengthening the role of Russian vocals. He believed that each note should reinforce the meaning of the words being sung. These principles were borne out in his opera, *The Stone Guest* (1872), based on the legend of Don Juan, and *Rusalka,* (1852) which was a great success and is still popular in Russia today.

After these two composers, the mood of nationalism in Russia grew ever more intense. The end of the Crimean war, the liberation of the peasants and the death of the Tsar Nicholas I, gave rise to a surge of creative power. The formation of a group of composers in the mid century, known as 'The Mighty Handful', led to a new productive period in the Nationalist school.

The Mighty Handful

The five composers who gave fresh impetus to Russian music were Balakirev (1837–1910, who wrote no opera, but who emerged as leader of the group), Borodin (1833–87), Cui (1835–1918), Mussorgsky (1839–1881) and Rimsky-Korsakov (1844–1908). Drawn together by great shared admiration for the works of Glinka, they built on the foundations that he and Dargomizhsky had laid. Among them they wrote a number of operas based on Russian themes.

Borodin's *Prince Igor* (1869–87) with its brilliant and famous *Polovtsian Dances,* is full of historical grandeur, noble gestures and lyricism; unfinished at Borodin's death, the opera was completed by his friends Alexander Glazunov and Rimsky-Korsakov, who worked on many of his colleagues' unfinished compositions.

None of the 'Handful' however, could match Mussorgsky's *Boris Gudunov* for originality and innovation. This masterpiece was based on a drama by the famous poet and thinker, Alexander Pushkin. It captures the very soul of Russia in its vigorous music and acute characterization. The work, though, was far ahead of its time. Mussorgsky's original was twice rejected by St Petersburg Opera, in 1868 and 1874. Apart from its rough and ready music, audiences were scandalized by its lack of heroine, and the large number of choruses.

After Mussorgsky's death, the work was extensively revised by Rimsky-Korsakov, who smoothed the rough edges, giving it a much more sophisticated orchestration. It is this version which has since been most often produced.

Mussorgsky's originality was the result of a conscious effort to avoid being part of any prevailing musical trend. Most of the 'Handful' shunned western influences (with the exception of Rimsky-Korsakov), but Mussorgsky went the furthest in his intuitive use of folk-inspired melody.

Of Rimsky-Korsakov's 14 operas, all but three are on Russian themes – folk tales, mythology or legends. They all show his gift for harmonic colour and orchestration. Like Glinka, he was drawn to themes dealing with the fantastic, the exotic, even the

Motley Books Ltd

Tchaikovsky's melodic gift, brilliant orchestration and the general accessibility of his music have made him Russia's most popular composer abroad.

The 20th century and Post-Revolutionary opera

With all this blossoming of talent in Russia, it was Sergei Diaghilev who showed its results in Europe. Today, Diaghilev is famous as the founder of the *Ballet Russes*. However he was first instrumental in introducing important Russian operas to both Paris and London. In 1907, he presented scenes from operas by Glinka, Mussorgsky and Rimsky-Korsakov at the Paris Opéra, and in 1908 the first full stage performance outside Russia of Mussorgsky's *Boris Godunov*, with Shalyapin. In 1913, the first Russian season was given at Drury Lane. A year later, in association with Sir Thomas Beecham, Diaghilev produced seven operas in London. Their originality and exoticism, coupled with powerful singing and acting, could hardly fail to make a deep impression on European audiences of the time.

One of the most spectacular operas given by Diaghilev was *The Nightingale* (1914) by a composer named Igor Stravinsky (1882–1971). This musical fairytale in three acts is based on a story by Hans Andersen and with this work, Stravinsky took Russian opera into the modern world. Of his later stage works, only *Mavra* (1922), based on Pushkin and reminiscent in style of the classical opera buffa, and his moral tale *The Rake's Progress* (1951), based on Hogarth's engravings, are conventionally operatic. All his other works question the traditional form of opera: *Les Noces* (1914–17) is more like ballets with songs and choruses and *Oedipus Rex* (1927) is an 'opera-oratorio'.

After the ravages of the 1917 Revolution in Russia, few principal composers remained in the Soviet Union. Sergei Prokofiev (1891–1953), however, returned after 20 years abroad. A brilliant and original mind, he wrote orchestral, chamber and piano music, as well as opera. His seven mature operas range from the stunning fairy-tale comedy, *The Love of Three Oranges* (1921), to a powerful expressionist drama, *The Fiery Angel* (first produced in 1954), also the epic based on Tolstoy's novel, *War and Peace* (1941–3, revised 1946–52). This opera, in five acts was finally cast in 13 scenes – the first seven scenes on peace, the last six on war.

However, the years after the Revolution were not an easy time for composers. The satirical mood of the 1920s which inspired Shostakovich's grotesque comedy, *The Nose,* written at the expense of the old Russia, was soon quashed. Under Stalin, music was supposed to appeal to the masses and be a means of educating them in useful socialist attitudes. In 1932 an artistic principle known as 'socialist realism' was formulated. Shostakovich's second opera, *Lady of Macbeth of Mtsensk,* was officially denounced for failing to express sufficiently 'the ideas and passions motivating Soviet heroes'.

Stalinism went on to oppose further works by Prokofiev but after Stalin's death, there was a general loosening of such strict artistic controls. The Revolution however, certainly helped to bring opera to the masses – there are now some 40 opera houses in the USSR. With the exception of *Boris Godunov,* though, few Russian operas have found a regular place in world repertories. But with Stravinsky, Prokofiev and Shostakovich, Russia has undoubtedly supplied some of the most important and influential operas seen in the 20th century.

The popularity of Boris Godunov *outside the Soviet Union owes much to the legendary performances in Paris (1908) of Russian bass Feodor Shalyapin (autographed photograph above) who immortalized the title role.*

The Fotomas Index

comic. His adventurous *Golden Cockerel,* a satire on the reign of Tsar Nicholas II, was banned druring his lifetime, not being produced until 1910, two years after his death. (Rimsky-Korsakov had sympathized with the cause of the 1905 revolution.) Based on a work by Pushkin of the same name, it has become his best known opera and won him world acclaim.

The invention and creativity of the 'Mighty Handful' meant that for a long time St Petersburg remained the centre of musical activity in Russia. Moscow, the older of the two cities, was hampered by a very provincial outlook on the arts and it was not until Tchaikovsky (1840–93) moved there, after his training in St Petersburg, that Moscow made an impact on Russian music.

Although Tchaikovsky knew the five members of the 'Handful' in St Petersburg, his differing musical tastes set him apart from them. Like them, he held Glinka in great esteem but despite this, he was primarily seduced by western music, especially that of Mozart. Of his ten operas, however, only *Eugene Onegin* (1879) and *The Queen of Spades* (1890) are frequently produced. *Eugene Onegin* is composed with great subtlety and perception, but his other works are dramatically weak. Nonetheless,

Chapter 11
Opera in England

*For centuries a slave to Italian dominance,
English opera was slow to claim its own identity.
The 20th century has revealed unique national
talent which has brought long-awaited success.*

Opera first came to England from Italy in the 17th century. In the following centuries repeated efforts were made by composers to establish a distinctively English style but this was not achieved until the 20th century. It was not that the English didn't take to opera: indeed, many were fascinated by the new art that had been devised by the Italians. Even before opera's arrival in England accounts of its splendour were brought back to Britain by travellers to the Continent.

It was in Venice, where at least 12 opera houses were built between 1637 and 1679, that the English diarist, John Evelyn, first saw opera. He noted:

This night we went to the Opera where plays are represented in recitative music by the most excellent musicians, vocal and instrumental, with a variety of scenes, and machines for flying in the air ... Taken together it is one of the most magnificent and extensive diversions the wit of man can invent.

The English, though, had their own tradition of extravagant entertainment. Elaborate masques had been, since Tudor days, a favourite royal pastime and

The first true English opera, Dido and Aeneas (1689) by Henry Purcell (above left), went unnoticed in its day, while Italian opera (above) became, and remained, all the rage in London's theatres.

had reached a new level of splendour during the reigns of the Stuarts. As diversions, these entertainments, in which music, dance, drama and spectacle were combined, were just as expensive to mount as Venetian operas. In addition, London now boasted theatres that, unlike the playhouse of Shakespeare's day, were roofed and had stages equipped with footlights and drop curtains. Artists

If there was one area of opera in which the English excelled, it was that of comic or ballad operas. John Gay's Beggar's Opera (1728, right) was the most popular of them all, and it was even given a new arrangement by Britten this century. Set in a prison, The Beggar's Opera is essentially a satirical work which lampoons famous contemporary politicians (including Walpole) as well as the very formal Italian operatic conventions and its singers.

William Hogarth 'The Beggar's Opera' Collection of Paul Mellon, USA/The Bridgeman Art Library

Mary Evans Picture Library

The forerunners of opera in England were the traditional court masques. Architect Inigo Jones (1573–1652) designed many of their elaborate sets and delightful costumes (above).

and designers such as Inigo Jones, who had travelled in Italy, provided sensational scenery and costumes. England, or rather its capital, liked stage productions that included singing, music and special effects, but audiences were not yet disposed to serious opera with continuous music after the Italian or French fashion.

Regarded as the first attempt at English opera, *The*

Siege of Rhodes (1656), with words by poet Sir William Davanant and music by M. Locke, H. Lawes and three lesser composers, does not survive. But it boasted a novelty in England as great as any of the Italian mechanical effects, in the shape of the first actress recorded to have appeared on the stage – a Mrs Coleman who sang the part of Ianthe. *The Siege of Rhodes* appears to have had no lasting effect on English taste, which continued to prefer its music to be diluted by spoken words.

Purcell's masterpiece

The first true opera arrived in 1689 in the form of Henry Purcell's *Dido and Aeneas.* Surprisingly though, this work, now recognized as Purcell's masterpiece, was intended not for theatre, but for a private performance by amateurs in a girls' boarding school in Chelsea. At the time, Purcell's work was overshadowed by the great popularity of extravagant spectacle of musical dramas – the public did not take to plays 'whereof every word is sung'.

There is no doubt, however, that Purcell had genius and his early death at the age of 36 was a tragedy for English opera. Had he lived he might well have been the man to succeed in establishing a native opera to match that of Italy and France. But the very strength of British dramatic traditions militated against a dominant role for music. In addition, there was a vigorous legacy of Puritanism. Just three years after Purcell's death a book entitled *A Short View of the Immorality and Profaneness of the English Stage,* by a writer named Jeremy Collier, appeared. In this overridingly critical work, Collier reserved particular ire for anything with operatic tendencies: 'This sort of Musick warms the Passions, and unlocks

the Fancy, and makes it open to Pleasure like a Flower to the Sun.'

The appearance of *A Short View* coincided with a decline in the production of English operatic work. From then on England took on the status of a 'poor relation' with regard to serious opera that was to last until the mid-20th century.

Italian opera in London

English audiences, however, were more tolerant of opera if it was in a foreign language and soon it was generally agreed that Italian was the 'natural' language for opera. By the 18th century Italian opera *was* opera in London.

In the 1720s the great German composer, Handel, became responsible for turning London into a major operatic centre. Profoundly influenced by his sojourns in Italy, he capitalized on the new fashion for Italian music, writing, within the opera seria convention, no less than 36 Italian-style operas for London. Many did well in 'box-office' terms, but in spite of his extraordinary output and flair, they were neither accepted by the Italians, nor did they manage to kindle the flame of English opera which had flickered briefly in the 17th century.

Handel's efforts might have had a more lasting effect on public taste had it not been for the strength of a rival British tradition — that of ballad operas, comic operas and burlesques, similar to the French *opéras comiques en vaudevilles* of about the same time. All of the action went ahead by the spoken word and the musical content took the form of incidental lyrics and various 'hit' songs.

In the 18th century a voracious appetite for light operas such as these was stimulated by the phenomenal success in 1728 of John Gay's *Beggar's Opera* — the most famous and popular of all ballad operas.

Besides being acted in London for 63 consecutive days, the *Beggar's Opera* was renewed the following season to even more applause. It then toured all the major cities and towns of the British Isles. In spite of this, by the end of the 18th century, even the general level of light opera had fallen, and, as far as serious opera was concerned, London audiences seemed content with their regular annual seasons of foreign operas, sung preferably by foreign singers in a foreign language.

For much of the 19th century the story was the

Built in 1732, London's original Covent Garden Theatre (above) housed, for many years, plays rather than operas. In 1808 the theatre was destroyed by fire, rebuilt, with an Italian-style opera interior in 1847 and razed again in 1856. It is only since the opening of the present building in 1858 that Covent Garden has become Britain's main operatic venue.

same. Rossini and, in due course, Verdi, enjoyed enthusiastic audiences. Then German opera, first the works of Mozart and eventually those of Wagner, also found a place in public esteem. Still Britain seemed to lack opera composers to match the genius of her poets and novelists. Even when native composers did produce suitable works, such strong foreign competition, together with a general lack of facilities, prevented British opera from building on its early foundations.

Irish composer Michael Balfe's (1808–1870)

Sir Michael Tippett (right) is today's most prominent British opera composer. Committed to exploring and exposing human nature, his King Priam (above) is a stark tragedy dealing with 'the mysterious nature of human choice'.

In the 20th century the cause of English opera was championed by Benjamin Britten (left). The success of his Peter Grimes in 1945 (below) at last brought English opera international recognition. Britten went on to write several other major operatic works and a wealth of music. Many of Britten's lead roles were created by his lifelong friend, the tenor Sir Peter Pears (far left).

Romantic opera, *The Bohemian Girl* (1843), became Britain's only serious international operatic success until the triumph of Benjamin Britten's *Peter Grimes* more than a century later. Balfe put his energy behind several schemes for a permanent English opera house, first at the Lyceum and then at Covent Garden. The Theatres Act of 1843 enabled the smaller theatres to put on straight plays without having to deck them out with songs, and then Covent Garden was free to concentrate on opera. Accordingly, it opened in 1847 with an interior redecorated along the lines of an Italian opera house and, despite rebuilding after fire in 1856, became London's premier opera venue. It was hoped that Covent Garden would receive some kind of state subsidy but the sudden death of Prince Albert in 1861, one of its most important supporters, put an

Zoë Dominic

end to this hope.

Composer Sir Arthur Sullivan (1842–1900) became the next great hope for English opera. Though renowned for the very successful operettas he produced in collaboration with the brilliant librettist William Schwenk Gilbert (1836–1911), Sullivan passionately wanted to write serious opera. In 1890, fortified by an expressed wish, virtually a command, from Queen Victoria, and the encouragement of his manager Richard D'Oyly Carte, Sullivan wrote his Grand Opera *Ivanhoe*. Hoping that this would spark off a series of similar operas, D'Oyly Carte built the 'Royal English Opera House' (now the Palace Theatre) in Cambridge Circus. But despite the popularity of *Ivanhoe,* which opened the theatre, the project soon foundered due to bad management.

From then until 1946, opera in England was left either to some syndicate to arrange an annual season of works in German, Italian and sometimes French at Covent Garden, or to companies such as the Carl Rosa (founded in 1875) which toured English versions of the more popular operas. During these fallow decades something like an English spirit of the 'people's opera' was growing up, first at the Old Vic Theatre, and then (after 1931) at Sadler's Wells in London. In addition to foreign operas, the Sadler's Wells Company presented homegrown productions, such as Charles Stanford's *The Travelling Companions,* Dame Ethel Smyth's *The Wreckers,* Gustav Holst's *Savitri* and Vaughan Williams' *Hugh the Drover.* The Second World War, however, halted these brave initiatives, and while Sadler's Wells

Zoë Dominic

became an evacuee centre, its much depleted company carried on, for as long as possible, with tours of the provinces.

Post-war triumphs

It is against this background of only isolated successes that the scale of Benjamin Britten's (1913–76) achievement must be measured. He wrote his first major operatic success, *Peter Grimes* (1944), for a country that still had no permanent opera company and no permanent opera house. In 1944 he declared:

I am passionately interested in seeing a successful permanent national opera in existence – successful both artistically and materially. And it must be vital and contemporary, too, and depend much less on imported 'stars' than on a first-rate, young and fresh, permanent company.

In 1945 it was agreed that Sadler's Wells would give *Peter Grimes* its first performance, marking the close of the war and the company's return to its de-requisitioned theatre. It was a resounding triumph, both at home and abroad, and it was an unmistakably British triumph. Britten lived in Aldeburgh on the Suffolk coast, and in 1948 he established an annual music festival that is still held there. It was a poem entitled *The Borough* by the Suffolk poet George Crabbe that had provided him with the theme for *Peter Grimes*. The opera tells the story of a man who takes boys from the local workhouse to be apprentices in his fishing business. It begins with the inquest on the death of Peter's first apprentice and ends with his downfall as another boy dies under suspicious circumstances and the people of the 'Borough' turn on Grimes as an anti-hero. The opera marked the beginning of Britten's career as an opera composer of world class, a career that was to continue with such masterpieces as *Billy Budd* (1951), *The Turn of the Screw* (1954) and *A Midsummer Night's Dream* (1960).

Britten's success encouraged other composers. In 1955, his friend and fellow composer, Michael Tippett (1905–) produced the lyrical and comic *The Midsummer Marriage*. Tippett has since completed three more strikingly original operatic works – *King Priam* (1962), *The Knot Garden* (1970) and *The Ice-Break* (1977).

Britten's achievement was buttressed by the foundation, in 1946, of a state-assisted permanent national opera company at the Royal Opera House, Covent Garden. In addition, Sadler's Wells went on to develop a stable opera company with a distinct emphasis on British singers who sang in English. The result was the formation of the English National Opera in 1974 which is permanently housed at the Coliseum, London.

Britten also had a deep concern for the music of Purcell: indeed, at times this amounted to a personal crusade. In writing *Peter Grimes* he had taken on the very spirit of Purcell, who had written three centuries earlier:

Poetry and Painting have arriv'd to their perfection in our own Country: Music is yet but a Nonage, forward Child which gives hope of what it may be hereafter in England, when the masters of it shall find more encouragement.

With the post-war renaissance of British opera, the legacy of Purcell was at last being realised.

GLYNDEBOURNE

A firework display in the grounds of the Glyndebourne estate – just one of the attractions that draws thousands of opera-lovers to the annual Festival every summer.

In 1931 a wealthy opera addict, John Christie, married the soprano Audrey Mildmay. Inspired by his wife, he built a small opera house in the grounds of his country estate at Glyndebourne, near Lewes in Sussex, and in May 1934 the annual Glyndebourne Opera Festival began.

Behind this realization of a personal dream however, was a very serious commitment to opera. Glyndebourne was to be the setting for foreign masterpieces sung in their original language and performed to the highest standards by an international cast. The operas of Mozart proved ideal, and performances of *Figaro* and *Cosi fan tutte* with Fritz Busch as conductor, Carl Ebert as producer and Rudolf Bing as general manager, soon put Glyndebourne on the map of the operatic world.

After the war, in 1946, Glyndebourne added English productions to its repertory and it gave Britten's first chamber opera, *The Rape of Lucretia,* followed by his *Albert Herring* in 1947. In 1954 the foundation of the Glyndebourne Arts Trust ensured the continuation of the Festival and after the 1953 production of Stravinsky's *Rake's Progress* the Glyndebourne company has had a strict policy of introducing at least one new work each season.

Not surprisingly, to hear opera so meticulously produced and in such an idyllic setting in the lap of the English South Downs means that Glyndebourne has been from the beginning an expensive, but unique experience.

Chapter 12
20th Century Opera

***Twentieth century composers gradually drew
away from Wagnerian tradition and produced
works full of experiment, deepening the
relevance of opera in society.***

At the start of the twentieth century there were signs that the towering influence of Richard Wagner was beginning to wane. Composers of opera were less and less inclined to follow the paths beaten by their predecessors. Each began to work out his own theory of what opera should be, the subjects it should treat, whether to have a specially written libretto or to draw from an existing play.

Claude Debussy (1862–1918) signalled an early break with Wagnerian tradition. An ardent Wagnerian in his youth, Debussy had made the pilgrimage to Bayreuth in 1882 to hear *Parsifal*. He later turned against his idol and in his only opera, *Pelléas et Mélisande* (1902), disappointed every existing operatic tradition. The work lacks any trace of Wagnerian rhetoric: Debussy's aesthetic affinities lay with French symbolist poets such as Mallarmé to whom rhetoric was anathema.

The opera is based on Maurice Maeterlinck's understated drama set in the mythical Allemonde, a country of dark forests peopled by characters who move as in a dream. It was an ideal text for Debussy. His score consists of short, musically linked scenes in which no more than a single fully formed melody can be discerned. The rest is all suggestion but of a powerfully gripping kind.

In Italy a tradition of sorts still obtained: that of 'verismo', the Italian equivalent of Zola's 'naturalism'. It first found expression in the low-life novels of Verga and Capuana, and it was Mascagni's Verga-based *Cavalleria Rusticana* (1890) that brought it into opera. It set a fashion that was to last two decades. On the one hand verismo was a revolt against the pomp and grandeur of works like Verdi's *Aida* and Ponchielli's *La Gioconda;* on the other it released a flood of romantic lyricism and rhetoric which opera's hitherto rather formal nature had precluded.

By 1900 verismo had come to denote not so much a social ambience as a musical style of swirling,

Set design by Stefanos Lazaridis for the 1985 production of Sir Michael Tippett's **The Midsummer Marriage**. *Influenced by the verse drama of T. S. Eliot, Tippett's comedy tells the story of two lovers facing unexpected hindrances on the road to marriage, problems based, the composer says, on 'our ignorance or illusion about ourselves.'*

emotionally charged melodies, full-blooded orchestration and much pictorial detail. Mascagni and his followers were all devotees of Wagner but they avoided Wagnerian length and took care to centre the interest on the voice; nor did they disdain the detachable solo, though cleverly woven into context.

Something new to say

The best works of these composers belong to the 1890s. Thereafter only Puccini, having already produced *La Bohème* (1896), *Tosca* (1900) and *Madam Butterfly* (1904), found something new to say. In his later works his style is much more concentrated, and enriched by influences absorbed from young contemporaries like Debussy and Stravinsky. Puccini's *Turandot,* first produced in 1926 after the composer's death, is one of the masterpieces of the century.

With the aid of authentic Chinese melodies Puccini creates a massive, colourful score in broad brush strokes. The tender hearted singer of 'little Italy' is present in the music of the tortured slave girl Liù. Only the failure to find the right note of sublimity for the denouement prevented Puccini finishing the work. The final two scenes were reconstructed from his sketches by Franco Alfano.

In Germany, Richard Strauss – 'Richard II' to his friends – made an orthodox Wagnerian debut but then shocked the world with *Salome* (1905). The opera is based on Oscar Wilde's 'decadent' play about the princess who dances before her stepfather, Herod Tetrarch, in return for the head of John the Baptist. Strauss uses all the resources of modern harmony and orchestral colouring to depict the corrupt sensuality of Herod's court but simple lyricism is never far below the surface: it informs both John the Baptist's music and even Salome's final orgy of necrophilia.

Harsher and more uncompromising is *Elektra* (1909) in which Strauss first collaborated with the poet Hugo Hofmannsthal, one of the great partnerships in operatic history. *Elektra* is a celebration of hatred and a lust for vengeance, glutted only when the heroine's brother Orestes has murdered their mother, Clytemnestra, and her lover. At the time its wealth of dissonant counterpoint seemed the epitome of everything avant-garde: nowadays the traditional train of thought beneath the opera's elaborate trappings is apparent.

The style of Strauss's major success, *Der Rosenkavalier* (1911), for all its romantic opulence, owes more to Strauss's other idol, Mozart, than to Wagner. The hero is a breeches rôle (the man is played by a woman), reflecting the composer's life-long love affair with the soprano voice. Never were female voices and orchestra more beautifully blended than in this opera.

After the more modest *Ariadne auf Naxos* (1912), a parable about fidelity, Strauss came to rely on craftsmanship rather than invention. (*Arabella,* 1933, which returns to Vienna, was unkindly dubbed by some Viennese 'Sclerosenkavalier'.) However, to the end Strauss could be relied upon to pour out an abundance of beguiling melody – 'as the cow gives milk', as the composer put it.

Schoenberg's 'Second Viennese School'

A very different attitude to the Wagnerian legacy was taken by the 'Second Viennese School' headed by Arnold Schoenberg. Their aim was to push back the

frontiers of tonality, continuing the direction taken by Wagner in *Tristan und Isolde.* Schoenberg belonged to the Vienna of Sigmund Freud and the expressionist painters Oskar Kokoschka and Richard Gerstl. The exploration of unconscious influences is strongly felt in his music.

The first operatic masterpiece of the school belongs to Schoenberg's pupil, Alban Berg. His *Wozzeck* (1925) is based on a play by Georg Büchner about a soldier who, bullied by his superiors and cuckolded by his sergeant-major, kills his faithless wife and then himself.

Almost atonal, *Wozzeck* is made up of short,

Richard Strauss's Salome *shocked the world when first shown (1970 Covent Garden production shown right). Below a scene from* Lulu, *Berg's unfinished opera. Prokofiev's* The Love for Three Oranges *(bottom) is a re-working of the* commedia dell'arte *atmosphere.*

musically linked, scenes in the manner of *Pelléas.* Each scene is cast in a separate form and each has a refined workmanship in which no single idea is repeated in the same form. For the first time in opera 'Sprechgesang' is used, a mixture of speech and song in which the notes are first pitched, then given an upward or downward inflexion according to their context.

For his second opera, *Lulu* (1937 posthumously), Berg used the 'twelve-note technique' pioneered by Schoenberg. In this an entire composition is based, horizontally and vertically, on permutations and combinations of a 'note row', that is, a particular arrangement of the twelve notes of the chromatic scale. The heroine is a femme fatale à la Carmen, one who without deliberate malice brings ruin to everyone she associates with. Society takes its revenge and she ends up in a London garret, then to be killed by Jack the Ripper. The final act of the opera remained in piano score at Berg's death in 1935 and it has only recently been completed by a competent hand.

Experiment and revolt

After 1918 a reaction against romanticism brought with it a taste for smaller forces, shorter forms, even a different relationship between text and music, in which the composer no longer aimed at enlarging upon the emotions of his characters. Paris saw a number of operatic experiments under the aegis of Jean Cocteau, notably Stravinsky's opera-oratorio *Oedipus Rex* (1927). Two years earlier Ravel's *L'Enfant et les Sortilèges* had it debut. In this, based on a story by Colette, a naughty child is taught a

Reg Wilson

lesson by the various pets and nursery objects he has maltreated – a cautionary child's tale for adults.

In Germany the free spirit of the Weimar Republic found operatic expression in the theatre of Bertholt Brecht and Kurt Weill. The two men collaborated on *The Threepenny Opera* (1928), an updated version of *The Beggar's Opera*. The new work was a revolt against the musical gourmandising of operas like *Der Rosenkavalier:* the score is lean and hard, with grimly ironic use of contemporary dance rhythms. A similar sleazy charm pervades Weill's *The Rise and Fall of the City of Mahagonny* (1930), a satire on the greed and selfishness of a capitalist society.

Archiv für Kunst und Geschichte

The Threepenny Opera, *with music by Kurt Weill, is a stark satire on capitalism. It established Bertholt Brecht's reputation.*

With the rise of the Nazis Weill's music was denounced as decadent and the composer was forced to emigrate. Brecht also fled Germany. Official favour now fell on the simplistic, dithyrambic operas of Carl Orff.

National operas based on folk idioms continued a fitful existence. Examples include Rimsky-Korsakov's *The Golden Cockerel* (1908), Vaughan Williams' *Hugh the Drover* (1914) and, on a more sophisticated level, Béla Bartók's *Duke Bluebeard's Castle* (1911, performed 1918).

The operas of Czech composer Leos Janácek belong in this category. He had his first success with *Jenufa* in 1904, a 'veristic' drama about a widow who drowns her stepdaughter's illegitimate baby to protect the girl's reputation. It is Janácek's later works, however, that are regarded as masterpieces. *Katia Kabanova* (1921), *The Macropulus Case* (1926) and *The House of the Dead* (1930 posthumously) are concise, vivid works of great dramatic force. Janácek's lyricism is nervous, often convulsive. The most tragic events are often despatched in a few off-hand bars rather than being dwelt on in flights of vocal melody. Audiences evidently like the approach: Janácek's works are consistently *the* success of the season in which they are performed.

The artist and society

Some twentieth century composers have used opera to put forward their own ideas of the artist's relation to society, often identifying themselves with some great figure from the past. Operas such as Pfitzner's *Palestrina* (1917), Hindemith's *Mathis der Maler* (1938), Schoenberg's *Moses und Aron* (1932, performed 1957) and Dallapiccola's *Ulisse* (1968) are all professions of faith and so contain their composer's most deeply-felt music, though not always the most accessible.

Both experimentation and tradition continued after the Second World War. Stravinsky's *The Rake's Progress* (1951) is an opera in English based on Hogarth's famous series of paintings. In it Stravinsky reveals a clear neo-classical vein, with echoes of Mozart and even passages of recitative with harpsichord. Poulenc's *Le Dialogue des Carmelites* (1957), about a group of nuns executed in the French revolution, is, in contrast, somewhat in the Debussy manner of understated drama.

Hans Werner Henze, born in 1926, is currently the dominant figure in German opera. His subjects include black comedy (*The Young Lord*, 1965), classical myth (*The Bassarids*, 1968) and political comment (*We Come to a River,* 1973).

In the United States, Deems Taylor's *The King's*

Henchmen (1927) and *Peter Ibbetson* (1931) were performed to critical acclaim at the time but have not been staged since. Gian Carlo Menotti's attempt to deal with contemporary problems in neo-Puccinian style had a passing success with *The Consul* (1950), but it is on his more modest works, like the Christmas opera *Amahl and the Night Visitors* (1951), that his reputation rests.

Samuel Barber's *Vanessa* (1958) and *Antony and Cleopatra* (1966) played to enthusiastic audiences in New York, the latter work opening the new Metropolitan Opera House. Perhaps the most enjoyable of all American operas is the exuberant *Porgy and Bess* by George Gershwin, with libretto by Edwin DuBose Heyward. It was coolly received when first performed in 1937 and it was not until 1942, five years after Gershwin's death, that an extensively re-worked version became a hit on Broadway. Leonard Bernstein's first opera, *Trouble in Tahiti* (1952), was also his last: his next work was the successful Broadway musical *West Side Story.*

Leading opera houses subsist mainly on a repertory of 'classics', many of them drastically re-interpreted by modern productions. Just as the age of the singer gave way to that of the conductor, the last thirty years have seen the producer in the ascendant. Wieland Wagner's well-nigh abstract *Ring*, Zeffirelli's realistic *Cavalleria Rusticana,* Visconti's historico-pictorial *Don Carlos,* Patrice Chéreau's jumble of heterogeneous symbols – the *Ring* again – are some of the most conspicuous examples of the modern producer's art.

A scene from Glyndebourne's 1975 production of Stravinsky's **The Rake's Progress.** *This opera, sung in English, is based on William Hogarth's series of paintings,* **The Rake's Progress** *(1735, Sóane Museum, London). The story tells of the sudden wealth, bankruptcy and eventual madness of Tom Rakewell.*

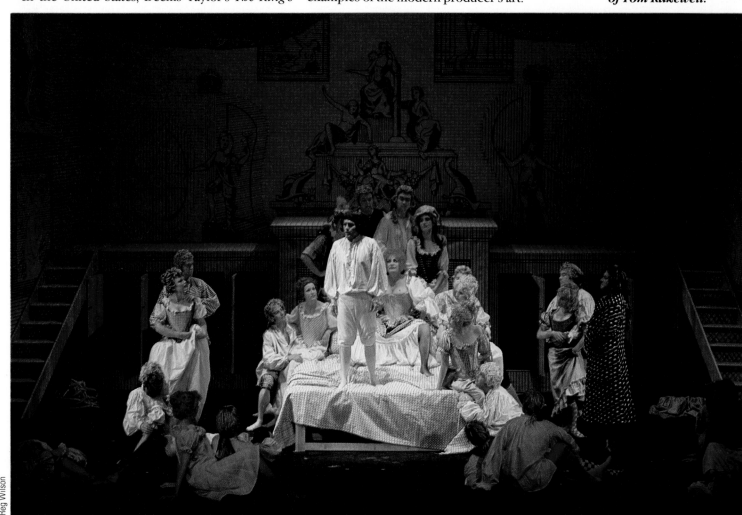

Chapter 13

Operetta

Comic plots, fast action, extravagant staging, infectious music . . . all part of the charm that has brought millions flocking to enjoy the light, frothy musical confections called operetta.

Operetta, light opera with comic plots, fast action, bright staging and infectious music, developed in the 1850s from French opéra comique, though the form had its antecedents in other countries: opera buffa in Italy, the zarzuela in Spain, in Germany and Austro-Hungary the Singspiel, in Britain the ballad opera.

Opéra comique (pages 23–6) had a distinguished lineage. Mozart's *The Marriage of Figaro* and *The Magic Flute* fused the sublime with the ridiculous and relied on a certain amount of buffoonery for their humour. Rossini and Donizetti brought gaiety and sparkle to opéra comique and had a tremendous influence: echoes of their works are to be found in the music of many leading operetta composers. It was Donizetti, for example, who introduced the military ensemble with a 'ra-ta-tat' refrain, later to become typical of operetta.

Offenbach: 'the Mozart of the Champs Elysées'

The great age of operetta – the word is the Italian diminutive of 'opera' – began in France in the 1850s when Jacques Offenbach (1819–1880) and others drew enthusiastic audiences to their musical confections. Offenbach had an eye for history: he liked to be known by the nickname given him by Rossini, 'the Mozart of the Champs Elysées'.

Offenbach was renowned for his speed, orchestrating his works at home amid the din of children and visitors. Such speed was achieved by the simple expedient of using material over and over again. (Franz Lehár did the same.) Offenbach's success was due partly to his music, partly to his skills as a businessman. He opened his own Theatre des Bouffes-Parisiens in the Champs Elysées in 1885. *Le Figaro* commented:

The title says everything about the repertoire. It is a theatre more than anything consecrated to openhearted laughter, to fantasy, to light and smart melody, to bold refrains.

Offenbach operas, such as *La Belle Helene, The Grand Duchess* and *Orpheus in the Underworld,* drew fashionable Paris as well as foreign heads of state. Such titles have stood the test of time: the more farcical operettas by other composers are scarcely remembered today. One plot centred on the exploits of a green parrot, another told the tale of a double bass player shipwrecked on a desert island with only a cannibal queen for company: he escapes in his double bass, using a handkerchief as a sail.

Such absurdities delighted audiences. They also gave ample opportunity for parody, and scope to lampoon opera. Much of the humour is lost on

Offenbach, shown below in an 1872 caricature, inspired many other musical pieces, such as Charles Coote's quadrille (left).

modern audiences. Offenbach is remembered just as much for one work which is not an opera – *The Tales of Hoffman* – as for any of his less serious works.

Operettas by other French composers now suffer similar obscurity. Bizet, Gounod, Massenet and

V. SARDOU. LE ROI CAROTTE J. OFFENBACH

Operetta depended for its success on lively spectacle performed by extravagantly attired actors (above).

Not everyone welcomed Offenbach's success (below). Some critics lamented what they saw as the 'naughtiness' of the French stage. Richard Wagner wasn't very charitable either: he attacked Offenbach's earlier works for having all 'the warmth of the dung heap'.

Chabrier all wrote operettas, none of which are performed today. Czech composer Antonin Dvořák, the only indisputably great composer since Mozart to distinguish himself in operetta and choral works, is not known for any of his ten operas, four of which may be classed as operettas. Dvořák wrote:

People see me only as a writer of symphonies but for many years I have demonstrated my liking for dramatic composition. I do not write opera from a desire for glory but because I consider it the most beneficial for the people.

Dvořák's operas, written in the 1870s, were based on Slavic history.

Vienna first staged pirated versions of Offenbach's works in the 1850s and the composer directed his own works there in the following decade. Local composers sought to emulate the French master: a work by Suppé, *Das Pensionat* (1860), is considered the first Viennese operetta. However, it was the first operetta by Johann Strauss the younger, *Indigo and the Forty Thieves* (1871), that began the Viennese challenge to French supremacy in operetta.

The rise of Viennese operetta

Strauss was already famous as the master of Viennese dance music and the translation of his acclaimed café waltzes to operetta was a logical step. Whether it was his idea or that of his more theatrically minded friends is a moot point: what is certain is that the story, which long held sway, that it was Offenbach himself who suggested the move, is no longer accepted.

Strauss's third operetta, *Die Fledermaus* (1874),

had all the ingredients likely to intoxicate Vienna: a sparkling plot, a great ball at the high point of the performance, every opportunity for captivating arias and waltzes. The first run of *Die Fledermaus* at the Theater an der Wein was frequently interrupted to make way for previously scheduled appearances by the famous singer, Adelina Patti. After the 49th performance the operetta was taken off because of illness among the cast. Two years later, after a triumphal run in Berlin, the work returned to Vienna and to enormous success. In Paris, the whole capital was soon dancing to the music of *Die Fledermaus*.

Strauss shared one problem with many other composers: how to find a good libretto. On the whole, operetta texts could be as incongruous, tasteless and as scatalogical as their author's chose to make them. As Beaumarchais, author of *The Marriage of Figaro,* noted: 'That which is too stupid to be spoken is sung'. Strauss was particularly unfortunate with his librettists. *Indigo* shows the scars of the 40 writers who worked on it. Even *Die Fledermaus* had six librettists.

For *The Gypsy Baron* (1885), his next great success, Strauss had just one librettist, who insisted that the music be composed first so that he could fit the words to it. This was a more successful approach. *The Gypsy Baron* is considered a more mature work than *Die Fledermaus*.

The Merry Widow

Strauss died in 1899, six years before the first performance of Franz Lehár's *The Merry Widow*. Like Dvořák, Lehár regarded operetta as a serious art form that should not be devalued by parody and burlesque. His plots were often absurdly romantic, his characters over-glamorised, but he did not draw in extraneous material for the sake of cheap laughs.

With Lehár, and the emergence of Romantic Viennese operetta, operetta achieved a new world-wide appeal. *The Merry Widow,* on one estimate, has been performed more than a quarter of a million times. It has been translated into 25 languages. It has been filmed, made into ballet, performed on ice.

What the contemporary Viennese public adored about the work were the lyric love songs but there

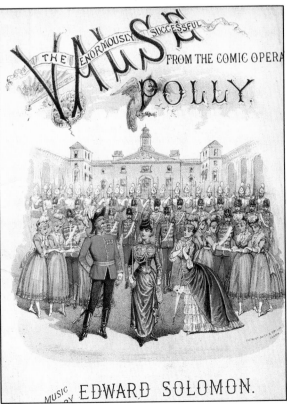

was, perhaps, a deeper reason for its popularity: *The Merry Widow* was of a glamorous era soon to be swept away by the century's first world war.

In the mid-1920s Lehár's collaboration with the leading tenor of the day, Richard Tauber, began. Particularly renowned for his roles in Mozartian opera, from 1925, when he appeared in Lehár's *The Land of Smiles,* Tauber became increasingly identified with light opera.

Tauber's success lay not only in the grandeur of his voice: he treated his material in a new, subtle way, from the first note establishing a rapport with the audience. When he was criticized for 'descending' to operetta he said adamantly: 'I'm not singing operetta, I'm singing Lehár.'

The admiration between composer and singer was

mutual. Lehár said of Tauber, 'We are brothers, without the luxury of blood relationship. Musically, with his all-embracing abilities, he stands far above his craft; as a heaven inspired singer he is master of the voice which I hear when I am composing; as a person he is the dearest grandest fellow.'

Between 1925 and 1934 Lehár produced six works which were far removed from the operetta ideal of Strauss or Offenbach. A biographer of Lehár has noted: 'If . . . operetta owes its continued existence to its capacity for revealing the plebian in every aristocrat, then Lehár's triumphs prove the reverse: that the better class operetta reveals the aristocrat hidden in every plebian.' This was the 'setting sun' of Viennesse operetta, setting a new standard for the genre's rebirth elsewhere.

The zarzuela

Spain had a rich national school of its own. The zarzuela, plays interspersed with songs and dances, began in the 17th century. The name derives from 'zarza', bramble bushes in the woods near Madrid where King Philip IV organised his royal enter-tainments. By the late 19th century it was a colourful affair, introducing bandits, bullfighters, bishops and other picaresque oddities. A feature of the zarzuela, which enhanced its appeal, was that the audience were invited to join in the refrains of popular songs and participate with the comedian in verbal exchanges — rather like the latterday music hall in Britain and the United States.

Gilbert and Sullivan

From the 1870s British operetta was dominated by

Songs and dances of the zarzuela (above), the exhilarating Spanish version of operetta, were as familiar to the Spanish people as the songs of Gilbert and Sullivan were to the English.

Edward Solomon, who wrote Billee Taylor *(1880, above left) and* Polly, *the unlikely saga of a green parrot (1882, bottom left), was one of Arthur Sullivan's most successful contemporaries. Solomon's music is generally in the English ballad or march style, with simple rhythms.*

W. S. Gilbert (right) and Arthur Sullivan (below), with publicity material for works based on two of their major successes. Sullivan wrote much music apart from comic opera: his tune for the hymn 'Onward Christian Soldiers' is perhaps best known, and his 'The Lost Chord' remains popular.

William Schwenck Gilbert (1836–1911) and Arthur Seymour Sullivan (1842–1900). Gilbert, the librettist and a lawyer by profession, first collaborated with Sullivan, England's leading composer of the day, in 1871 but their comic opera *Thespis* met with little success. They were brought together again in 1875 by Richard D'Oyle Carte and the result, *Trial by Jury,* first staged as an afterpiece to an Offenbach operetta, ran for more than a year.

The Sorcerer (1877) and *HMS Pinafore* (1878) were performed by the Comedy Opera Company, formed by D'Oyly Carte specifically to stage full length Gilbert and Sullivan operettas. While *Patience* (1881) was still running, D'Oyly Carte moved to his newly-built Savoy Theatre. Later Gilbert and Sullivan works became known as 'the Savoy Operas': *Iolanthe* (1882), *Princess Ida* (1884), *The Mikado* (1885), *Ruddigore* (1887), *The Yeoman of the Guard* (1888), and *The Gondoliers* (1889).

Gilbert and Sullivan were an unlikely partnership: Sullivan was ingratiating, sociable, charming; Gilbert irascible, witty, unforgiving. Their relationship was to end in rancour, but not before they had produced works which, 100 years on, can still be relied on to draw capacity audiences throughout the English-speaking world.

They were perhaps the first team to give equal weight to the words and the music: not deliberately – Sullivan often felt his music took second place to Gilbert's words – but as the finished work appeared to audiences. Much of their success lay in the fact

that they appealed to Victorian morality. Gilbert wrote of French operetta:

The plots had generally been bowdlerised out of intelligibility, and when they had not been subjected to this treatment they were frankly improper . . . We resolved that our plots, however ridiculous, should be coherent, that our dialogue should be void of offence and that no man should play a woman's part, and no woman a man's.

Victorians, many of whom had been brought up to regard playhouses or theatres as dens of vice, flocked to see and hear Gilbert and Sullivan's comedies.

The plots are sedate and gentlemanly, the libretti full of good humour. There are witty asides about other composers and tongue-in-cheek disparagements of British institutions, but it is understated, without the satire and political references of French operetta. The humour relies much on irony – and on Gilbert's determination to treat a ridiculous notion with the utmost seriousness.

Today's audiences are used to elaborate stage presentation but when *The Mikado* was first performed good production was relatively new. Gilbert had costumes designed at Liberty's, and engaged a Japanese lady to teach the cast fan manipulation, mannerisms and deportment. All this was good publicity for an operetta that still delights international audiences.

Gilbert and Sullivan had an inestimable influence on British and American musical theatre, entrenching tastes in the Edwardian era until Noel Coward's musical plays came into vogue in the 1930s. Twentieth century works like *The Sound of Music, West Side Story, My Fair Lady, Evita,* are all popular musical plays. Though nobody calls them operettas, they carry on the tradition of word and song dramas that have enthralled audiences for centuries.

Great opera houses

It is difficult to imagine opera being performed outside large, purpose-built theatres, but early opera did not need opera houses. The earliest known opera, Dafne (1598), was performed in the home of one of its composers, and Monteverdi's Orfeo (1607) – the first great opera – was performed in a small room at the court of the Duke of Mantua where Monteverdi was Court Musician. However, as opera's audiences grew and performances required increasingly complex stage machinery, special buildings became essential. The Teatro San Cassiano, the first public opera house, was opened in Venice in 1637 and, as opera's popularity spread across Europe, opera houses were built in other cities: the Royal Opera House was opened in London's Covent Garden in 1732 and Milan's Teatro alla Scala (La Scala) followed in 1778. Today most large cities have an opera house where performances of opera, ballet and other large-scale theatrical works can be held.

Metropolitan Opera House, New York

The Metropolitan Opera House, with its joyous Chagall murals, dominates Lincoln Centre. It opened in September 1966 with, unfortunately, a disastrous première of Barber's Antony and Cleopatra. Originally sited on Broadway, the Metropolitan Opera was founded in 1883 by 20 millionaires who could not acquire boxes at the Academy of Music, where most opera performances were held. It opened then with Gounod's Faust and has had a distinguished history since, presenting nearly every famous singer and many eminent conductors.

Brian Delf

War Memorial Opera House, San Francisco

The great opera house in San Francisco is not quite the grand building that one expects. In fact, it is relatively new (1932), part of a sober civic complex and dedicated as a war memorial. Nonetheless, it houses one of the world's greatest companies and embodies a traditional love of opera that stretches well back into the last century. In earlier days, Jenny Lind and Adelina Patti were among the stars to travel to San Francisco, while the great Caruso was singing there shortly before the disastrous earthquake of 1906.

Brian Delf

Royal Opera House, Covent Garden, London

One of the world's best known opera houses, London's Covent Garden dates back to 1732 and has played host to many of the world's great singers from Luigi Lablache to Placido Domingo. The present building, home of the Royal Opera, was opened on 15 May 1858 and seats over 2,000 people.

Brian Delf

Glyndebourne, England

Once, servants waited on the patrons in the dining hall: now helicopters disgorge the new industrial élite with their mandatory picnics on the lawns of Glyndebourne in Sussex. Home of the Glyndebourne Festival Opera, this institution was the brain-child of an ex-Eton schoolmaster, John Christie, one of whose aims was to provide 'good opera at high prices rather than bad opera at low prices'. As each heavily over-subscribed season proves, it is extremely good opera that is provided briefly each summer in this unlikely but idyllic setting in rural England.

Brian Delf

Staatsoper, Vienna

With the fall of the Austro-Hungarian Empire, the Imperial and Royal Court Opera became the Vienna Staatsoper. After a stormy period leading up to its opening in 1869, which drove one of its designers (Van der Null) to suicide, the Staatsoper began to carve out a fine reputation which it still enjoys. In WWII the building was partly destroyed by bombs and was later rebuilt, but the outer walls are all original.

Brian Delf

The Volksoper, Vienna

Famous for its production of Viennese operetta, the Volksoper serves as Vienna's second opera house; however, it began life as the Kaiserjubilaüms Stadttheater, built to celebrate the golden jubilee of Franze Jozef's reign in 1898. It acquired its present name in 1903. Though located in a more modest part of Vienna than the Staatsoper, the Volksoper successfully staged the State Opera's productions while the latter was closed because of war-time bombing during 1945–55. The Volksoper continued to share the opera season with the Staatsoper and the Theater an der Wien until 1955 when it began to expand its operetta repertoire. The 1970s modernization included the removal of what had come to be known as Hitler's box.

Brian Delf

The Festival Theatre, Bayreuth

The foundation stone of the Festival Theatre was laid in 1872 – the same year that
Wagner settled in the Bavarian town. Designed specifically with Wagner's operas in
mind, the theatre opened in 1876 with a performance of the complete Ring cycle.
Following Wagner's death in 1883, the theatre became a place of pilgrimage for lovers
of Wagner's music, and from 1951 to 1966 the theatre was under the artistic direction
of Wagner's grandsons, Wolfgang and Wieland. Since 1966 Wolfgang Wagner has been
the sole artistic director.

Brian Delf

Nationaltheater, Munich

Originally known as the Hof und Nationaltheater, the Nationaltheater is home of the Bavarian State Opera company. Modelled on the Paris Odéon, the theatre opened in 1818 and proved so popular that, after a fire destroyed it, the population subsidised its rebuilding to the original design through a special beer levy. The best of German conductors, including von Bülow, Knappertsbusch, Leitner, and Kempe have been its directors – and the best of German operas, by Mozart, Strauss and, of course, Wagner feature strongly in performances.

Brian Delf

Grosses Festspielhaus, Salzburg

The summer festival at Salzburg, in the delightful setting of Mozart's birthplace, has been held since 1920 and gives special emphasis to Mozart's music. Under eminent conductors such as Walter, Toscanini and Furtwängler, the festival reached its zenith in the 1930s. Major opera productions are presented at the Grosses Festspielhaus (the Great Festival Theatre) which opened in 1960 with Der Rosenkavalier conducted by Herbert von Karajan. The theatre occupies the site of the stables of the former Winter Riding School and retains its original facade. The Müchsberg mountain which it abuts had to be blasted into a distance of 50 feet to accommodate one of the world's largest stages.

Brian Delf

Bolshoi Theatre, Moscow

Even before the Revolution, Russians of all classes enjoyed opera. Along with the Kirov in Leningrad, Moscow's Bolshoi ranks among the best opera houses of the world. The Bolshoi – literally 'grand' (and truly, given its massive proportions and ornate gilding) – opened in 1825. As seems the melancholy habit of opera houses, it later burnt down, to be re-opened in 1856. The premiéres of many late-19th-century Russian operas were given there, with characteristically lavish productions of mass crowds and elaborate sets. Since the Second World War, many other world-famous opera companies, including those of Covent Garden, La Scala and the Vienna Staatsoper, have visited Moscow.

Brian Delf

Palais Garnier, Paris

One of the grandest theatre houses in the world, the magnificent Palais Garnier (more commonly known simply as L'Opéra) has housed the Paris opera since its completion and opening on 5th January 1875. Designed by Charles Garnier it also boasts the world's largest stage (100 feet by 112 feet) and a vast 2000 seat auditorium.

Brian Delf

Teatro alla Scala, Milan

From Rossini to Puccini, every great Italian composer has written for The Teatro alla Scala (La Scala). Built in 1778, it was named after the Duchess of Visconti (part of whose name was La Scala) who had founded a church on the site in the 14th century. By the mid-19th century, La Scala was one of the leading opera houses in Europe, setting new standards especially in stage design. In 1920, the theatre came under the artistic direction of Toscanini and it enjoyed its most glorious period. Maria Callas's presence in the 1950s contributed to a revival of long-forgotten bel-canto operas. It seats 3,000, and afficionados claim that the best sound is to be heard in the cheapest seats in the gallery.

Brian Delf

The Sydney Opera House

In 1973, Queen Elizabeth II officially opened the Sydney Opera House, part of a large arts complex attesting to Australia's pride in its artistic credentials. The result of an international competition won by a Danish architect, its then controversial structure on the harbour is now a well-known symbol throughout the world. The Sydney Opera House is the home of Australian Opera, which with the partnership of Dame Joan Sutherland and her husband, Richard Bonyage – its director since 1976 – has achieved considerable international status.

Brian Delf

Understanding opera

Like most complex human creations, opera is more enjoyable if its rules, conventions and special language are understood. The following pages begin by describing those conventions that are fundamental to opera and make it unique: for example, the aria, the libretto and the recitative. Early in its history, opera's nature as a drama in which the words are spoken rather than sung led to the emergence of 'stars' – singers who attracted a fanatical following. Though modern fans may be less demonstrative, opera still depends on superb male and female singers, and pages 76-9 discuss the male and female voice and describe some great modern singers. The plot often seems peripheral to opera, but understanding the action obviously makes the performance more comprehensible, so pages 81-4 recount the plots of some of the most frequently performed operas. A glossary and bibliography completes this guide to understanding opera.

A guide to operatic conventions

The aria

Aria, Italian for 'air' or song, is a richly expressive song, sung nearly always solo, by the leading characters in an opera. First introduced by the early Italian composers

Kiri te Kanawa (above) singing the Jewel Song aria in Gounod's opera, Faust.

of opera in the 16th century, the aria's original function was to provide a break from the continual dramatic action and to allow the main characters to express, in an intensely lyrical way, their personal reaction to the narrative. The aria therefore provided a contrast to the 'recitative' – or the passages of sung narrative, – with points of deeper contemplation by the leading characters.

The aria, once introduced, dominated opera for hundreds of years, and throughout its history, like opera itself, was subject to continual change and development.

Monteverdi, in his work *Orfeo* (1607), was one of the first great composers of opera to use simple aria forms. By the time he wrote the *Coronation of Poppea* (1642) his arias had already become more complex, resembling in fact, an early type of the *Da Capo* aria which was to become the standard form used by composers for more than a century. 'Da capo' means literally, 'from the head' or 'back to the beginning' and the *Da Capo* aria was usually in three parts, beginning first with one tune and in one key, then changing to another tune and another key, before a repeat of the first section, repeated usually with some ornamentation.

It was Alessandro Scarlatti who developed the *Da Capo* aria into a strictly organized shape and it became, between 1650 and 1750, almost suffocating in its convention. At this time there were often as many as 30 to 50 arias in each opera with the basic formula being elaborated upon to accommodate a number of standard themes.

From this, though, at least 15 different aria types emerged – an aria for every occasion.

There were arias tailored to express a whole host of emotions, the *aria di sentimento* (sentimental aria), the *aria di agitato* (or agitation), arias of love, hate or jealousy etc. There was even an aria designed to allow the singer to leave the stage – the *aria di sortita*.

In the first half of the 18th century arias became, first and foremost, the means by which singers could display their vocal virtuosity. Most had a *cadenza* at the end, a florid unaccompanied passage to show off the range and agility of the voice.

The 19th century saw a general reduction in the numbers of arias and their style also became freer. Rondo arias appeared and cabalettas – in which there were changes of speed within the aria. Under Verdi, the giant of Italian opera, arias became much more intense and more powerful than before, pushing the singers to the limits of their vocal range and powers of emotional expression. The loosening of the aria's form continued throughout the 19th century, until in Wagner's works, for example, they became almost indistinguishable from the main part of the opera.

20th century composers like Hindemith, Schoenberg and Stravinsky reinstated classical forms of arias in their operas but, as a whole, the modern tendency has been towards the complete omission of the aria in favour of the more highly integrated form of sung-theatre.

The chorus

The chorus, along with the aria, recitative and the ensemble, is one of the basic features of opera. It is usually made up of a combination of male and female voices – the soprano, contralto, tenor and bass – though it may consist entirely of male or female, even children's, voices and the number and strength of these can be varied according to the required effect.

In ancient Greece, the *Khoros* was a group of dancers or singers and an important part of tragedy plays. The earliest operas in Italy were very much based on ancient Greek drama and therefore gave an important role to the chorus. Composers, especially Monteverdi, used it not only to comment on the plots of their operas as they unfolded, but also to provide an important contrast to long sections of solo singing. In addition, it was a useful formal device to bring acts to a close, with composers reserving especially spectacular arrangements for the ends of works. The chorus flourished in France in the 17th and 18th centuries in the works of Lully and Rameau where it became increasingly lavish and began to take on more dramatic importance.

It was in the second half of the 18th century, however, that the role of the chorus in opera radically changed. Among

The Soldiers' Chorus in Gounod's Faust (below) replaced the drinking song.

73

the many reforms made by Gluck was the integration of the chorus in the drama. Gluck used the members to make up crowd scenes on the stage, as for instance, groups of courtiers, nobles, slaves, priests, to improve the realism of opera as drama.

This move gave the chorus a whole new range of possibilities in opera. As the 19th century progressed, and rich romantic operas evolved, it became an even stronger feature. For example, Verdi's famous 'Anvil' chorus in Act II of *Il Trovatore* is employed to set the scene of a gypsy encampment, with all the gypsies singing together to the sound of their beating anvils. Even more spectacular is Verdi's chorus in Act II of *Aida* in the scene of the grand march. In this complex scene, all the main characters make an appearance, while the chorus divides to represent three groups, the slaves and prisoners, singing of their oppression, the priests, calling for the death of the vanquished Ethiopians and the populace who are praising King and country with the triumphal chorus, 'Gloria all'Egitto'.

The chorus then, in the 19th century, was used in a variety of ways – it could comment on the action, set a scene and play an active role in the drama.

Wagner, who set his own musical conventions, made various uses of the chorus. In *Tristan* (1865) and *The Ring* (1876) it makes only fleeting appearances, while at other times its role is more than ever involved with dramatic content, for instance, in his *Mastersingers of Nuremburg* (1868), where the citizens of Nuremburg are an intrinsic part of the opera's plot. This tendency for the chorus to be increasingly linked with the drama had continued into the 20th century. Benjamin Britten's *Peter Grimes* (1945) has a chorus of townspeople who make up the collective voice accusing the hero, and this is the main dramatic force pitted against him throughout the opera.

Stravinsky, on the other hand, in his neo-classical works, not surprisingly reverts to the ancient Greek style, using the chorus to comment on the drama. In his *Oedipus Rex* (1927) the chorus is set apart from the soloists as they lament the plague, pray to the gods, and echo and heighten Oedipus' agony. With Stravinsky, therefore, the function of the chorus turns full circle.

The duet

The duet is a piece for two singers and it has been one of the basic elements of opera from its early beginnings in the 17th century. A duet had a very flexible structure and may be sung by any combination of the sexes, singing either together, in harmony, unison or in dialogue. Duets, therefore, may be sung by friends, lovers or deadly rivals and as with arias are usually set for moments of heightened emotion in the plot. Due to their lyrical musical

The duet Tornami a dir *performed by Ernesto and Norina from* Don Pasquale *by Donizetti.*

quality many great duets have become firm favourites among opera goers.

Monteverdi was the first composer of opera to use the duet, and the finale of his *Incoronazione di Poppea* (1642) set the pattern for duets for two centuries after. In the 19th century however, with composers such as Verdi and Puccini, the duet, like the aria, became less clear cut, and merged into the general continuity of the music.

With Wagner, the duet found a new champion and in his *Tristan und Isolde* (1865) for example, most of the second act is taken up by an intense musical dialogue between the two lovers.

The love duet has always been the most popular form with composers. Mozart wrote several and his *Magic Flute* (1791) included the famous semi-comic duet between Papagena and Papageno, as well as the more spiritual one by Tamino and Pamina, 'Wir wandelten durch Feuergluten'.

More familiar are the great love duets of the 19th-century Romantic operas. Among the many that Verdi wrote, are the two in Act 1 of *La Traviata* (1853) – 'Libiamo ne'lieta', which is in part a drinking song, in which Alfredo, the guest, sings lines, which his hostess takes up before the chorus also joins in. The second is the beautiful declaration of love by Alfredo 'Un di felice' to which Violetta responds with equal rapture. Another of Verdi's most famous love duets is that of Otello and Desdemona, 'Gia nella notte' which comes at the end of the first act of *Otello* (1887).

Many other duets are to be found in

opera, apart from those between lovers. Some are between two friends as is the duet 'Au fond du temple saint' from Bizet's *Pearl Fishers,* sung by the contrasting voices of a tenor and a baritone – two friends who love the same woman, but recall their oath of friendship.

The flower duet 'Scuoti quella fronda' sung by Butterfly and Suzuki at the end of Act II in Madam Butterfly on the other hand, combines the voices of the soprano and mezzo as does another famous flower duet, 'Dôme épais, le jasmin', from Delibes' *Lakmé* (1883) in which Lakmé and Mallika muse on the beauty of the flowers in the morning light, before the main drama of the opera begins. Much of this duet is sung in thirds – or three notes or tones apart – and this device gives a particularly pleasing harmony.

Rivalry between lovers or others is also a common cause for an operatic duet. There is for example, the famous encounter between Otello and Iago. Iago has poisoned Otello's mind against Desdemona, out of sheer jealousy and hatred. In 'Si pel Ciel', Otello threatens to raise his hand in rage, then Iago, joining in the impassioned duet, vows to dedicate himself to his master as long as he will carry out his will.

Themes of friendship, rivalry and love can be traced through many of the operas of the 20th century, but there has been no new use of the duet: often, traditional techniques are simply inserted into the music of new composers. Even so, the duet remains un-challenged as one of the mainstays of opera.

The ensemble

Ensemble is simply the French word meaning 'together' and, in opera, it applies to any situation where soloists come together in duet, trio, quartet, quintet, sextet etc. The ensemble has become, with the aria, recitative and chorus, one of opera's basic ingredients.

In the majority of cases, the ensemble is characterized by each singer simultaneously following individual vocal lines which have been skillfully woven together by the composer so that the listener hears each one separately. On occasions, however, characters may sing together in unison but this is usually for some specific formal effect, such as to round off a scene or act. Although the function of the ensemble is different to that of the chorus, at times the two are used in conjunction – either to close an act or to end an opera.

The ensemble seems to have been introduced in the earliest Italian operas developing as a permanent feature by the beginning of the 18th century and resembling the aria in that it was normally reflective in nature. The first French composers of opera, Lully and Rameau, produced works with much more complex writing and their ensembles were often much longer and taken at a more energetic pace – often exhausting the singers in the process. They also used the ensemble, in addition to recitative, to forward the action and this technique eventually became universal. Soon the ensemble was found to be a particularly useful tool in comic opera as it enabled characters to break out more easily into humorous dialogue or discussion. During the 18th and 19th centuries it became a very popular device – by varying both the emotional strands and the voice pitches of the characters, composers could create some beautiful set pieces in either tragic or comic situations. A fine example is a quartet from the first act of Beethoven's *Fidelio* between Fidelio, Marzelline, Rocco and Jaquino. Marzelline sings that she thinks Fidelio is in love with her. Fidelio, really a woman (Leonore), forsees the problems that this will create. Meanwhile Rocco expresses his hope that they will make a happy couple, while Jaquino is in despair because he himself loves Marzelline. Ensembles therefore, in addition to being aurally pleasing, can also deftly express both dramatic irony and comedy arising out of misunderstanding.

The ensemble was also very skilfully employed by Mozart whose *Don Giovanni* (1787) ends with a lively sextet – after the Don has been consumed by flames and all the other characters have explained their intended course of action, they all join together for a moralizing final verse.

Verdi made much more extensive use of the ensemble, as is brilliantly shown in his final opera, *Falstaff* (1893), where the device becomes fully integrated with the musical flow while helping to forward the action and develop character. Act I scene II ends with a whirling nonet and, although nine voices are not easy to follow clearly, the humorous and playful effect Verdi seeks to produce is successfully achieved.

Wagner, in his *Die Meistersinger von Nurnberg* (1868), shows an example of a quintet of characters expressing their ideas in harmony, but on the whole he steered away from the ensemble, as he did the use of other such formal techniques.

In general however, modern composers of opera have favoured the continued use of the ensemble, with composers like Debussy, Schoenberg and Werner Henze employing it in various forms, despite their often revolutionary style.

The libretto

The libretto is the text of the opera, the words that the composer sets to music and which the singer has to learn. Librettos are the raw materials of opera but are often overlooked in favour of the music, the staging and the performers.

Libretto is Italian for 'little book'. The first libretti, printed privately for Italian nobles, were 20cm high, but became

The poet and celebrated librettist, Lorenzo da Ponte (above). He worked with Wolfgang Amadeus Mozart at court in Vienna, and together they produced works such as The Marriage of Figaro, Don Giovanni *and* Cosi fan tutte.

standardized to about 15cm – a convenient pocket size. The title pages of librettos would bear the emblem of the patron of the work, together with the name of the librettist, impresario and printer, but not necessarily the composer. The actual text was preceded by the *argomento*, which set the scene for the opening of the opera, and a few words at the end assured listeners that the author was still a faithful Christian – due to the often pagan subject matter of the work!

The libretto serves as the composer's inspiration and as such its main requirement is that it must be a dramatic story, as well as being adaptable to the demands of music drama. In the past, librettists were usually playwrights or poets, their sources drawn from a wide range, including classical myths, heroic legends, great dramatic works or novels from literature, poems or history itself.

The first libretto was written by Rinuccini for Peri's *Dafne* (1597) and since then approximately 30,000 have followed. At first it was common for the librettist to write without consulting the composer who would write the score – the best librettos were simply printed and then used time and time again as different composers set the same words to new music. Apostolo Zeno (1668–1750) and Carlo Goldoni (1707–1793) were two of the most popular authors of opera texts in the 18th century, but the real giant was the Italian Pietro Metastasio (1698–1782) who had 27 of his works set to music, up to 1000 times by at least 50 composers.

Eventually, though, composers found close collaboration with a single librettist a much more satisfactory arrangement and thus many fine partnerships emerged. Among these have been Lully and Quinault, Gluck and Calzabigi; Mozart and Lorenzo Da Ponte. Verdi had a closer colleague, Ariggo Boito: his libretto for Verdi's *Otello* is one of the finest in all opera. Shakespeare's text is compressed, but its conciseness gives it a new power and vigour. Boito and Verdi also produced the tight and brilliant comedy *Falstaff*.

Another successful partnership was that of Richard Strauss and Hugo von Hofmannsthal. Strauss had made an attempt to write his own texts, but after working with Hofmannsthal on *Elektra,* they went on to produce five more works together.

For some composers, even close collaboration with a librettist was not enough to produce the real unity of words and music that they sought, and they chose to write their own texts. Wagner wrote the librettos for most of his works, including *Der Ring des Nibelungen, Tristan* and *Parsifal* as did Berlioz and Mussorgsky. Since their time, many have done the same, including Pfitzner, Hindemith, Schoenberg, Shostakovich and Tippett.

In time past, opera audiences would buy the libretti of operas they wanted to see – even learn by heart their favourite passages. Today, not every opera-goer wishes to have a printed libretto to hand and most people content themselves with reading a synopsis of events in the programme notes. Even so, familiarity with the text enriches every opera visit.

The overture

The term *overture* comes from the French word *ouverture* meaning 'opening'. When used in relation to opera, it refers to the orchestral introduction to a work. The term *prelude* may sometimes be substituted for 'overture', though this may imply a shorter form, and may also run into the first scene of the opera.

Operatic overtures have varied considerably in form throughout history. They stem from the first brass fanfares or flourishes of trumpets that the earliest composers of operas used to inform their audiences that performance was about to begin. However, these rapidly became more elaborate and by 1607, Monteverdi's *Orfeo* had a longer opening, in toccata form.

As overtures became more popular with composers, different types emerged, notably the *French* and *Italian overtures*. By the 18th century, most operas began with one or other of these standard forms. Their use was not confined to national boundaries, though, and they were only so-called after the countries of origin.

The *French overture* was developed in the 17th century by Lully. It invariably had three sections: a slow, grand introduction, a fast central section and a slower final part – usually some sort of dance, such as a gavotte or a minuet. The music had no connection with the music in the opera, but was simply an introductory piece.

The *Italian overture,* or *sinfonia* as it was called, was developed by Alessandro Scarlatti in the early 18th century. Generally more brilliant than its French counterpart, it also had three parts arranged in a fast, slow, fast sequence, although later in the century, the second and third parts were usually omitted. This type usually introduced opera buffa.

The French composer Rameau was the first to use material taken from the actual opera in the overture – in his *Castor et Pollux* (1735). But later in the century, Gluck also used the overture to prepare the audiences for the dramas to ensue. Mozart continued the practice, writing mainly in sonata form, with his overtures incorporating several of the musical ideas from the main part of the accompanying opera. In addition, many of Mozart's overtures ran straight into the first scenes.

Four of the best known of all overtures were written by Beethoven for his *Fidelio.* The first three that he wrote, known as *Leonore Nos. 1, 2* and *3,* were considered by him to be too powerful, so he replaced them with a single overture called *Fidelio.*

Weber took the idea of 'summing up' an opera in its overture even further – in his *Der Freischutz* virtually every theme which appears in the overture, reappears as the opera unfolds. Some 19th-century composers of opéra comique and operetta, such as Auber, Gounod, Offenbach and J. Strauss, wrote overtures that were a *pot-pourri* (or medley) of their opera tunes.

Other composers, however, limited their overtures to a few preceding bars, or, in the case of some of Verdi's, Puccini's or Richard Strauss' works, they had none at all.

Wagner placed great importance on the overture. For him they were vital in preparing his audiences psychologically and emotionally for the huge works that were to follow. Later he came to prefer the shorter *Vorspiel* (prelude). Most run straight into the opening of the dramas.

Recitative

The word *recitative* comes from the Latin *recitare,* which means 'to read' or 'to recite'. In opera, it is the name given to the sung, half-sung or spoken declamatory passages which link the arias, duets and choruses. Recitative, which often follows the rhythm and accentuation of speech, is an essential part of opera because it keeps the audience informed as to what is going on in the story and, therefore, helps advance the plot. It also has the function of providing a contrast with the most intensely lyrical passages, such as the arias, and, therefore, provides a relief in tension from their high emotional pitch. Recitative

is often regarded with some impatience, not only by the audience but sometimes by the singers themselves, some of whom have a tendency to rush through it and on to the arias where they can better display their vocal talents. Audiences too, may also find recitative passages sung in foreign languages musically dull, compared to the great arias. But from the 16th century to the end of the 19th century, recitative has played an important role in opera.

In the first operas of the late 16th and early 17th centuries, recitative formed a substantial part of the works but there was no real distinction from the more melodic passages. This distinction, however, became increasingly clear-cut during the course of the 17th century – as the aria grew in importance, so passages of recitative became merely functional, matter-of-fact transitions between the arias that dominated the works.

In the 18th century, the form of recitative most commonly used was *recitativo secco* (or dry recitative). In this form, the recitative was delivered with no melody or tune for the singer to follow, only a sparse accompaniment on the harpsichord, or perhaps the cello, with chords being played to suit the verbal stress of the lines. The idea of this light accompaniment was to allow the audience to follow clearly the

singers' words. This style was widely used by Mozart, for example in *Cosi Fan Tutte* (1790) and *Don Giovanni* (1787) and later revived by Rossini in his 19th century *Barber of Seville* (1816).

Another widely used form of recitative is *recitativo accompagnato* or *stromentato,* employed by the great Italian opera composers of the 19th century, such as Donizetti and Verdi. Accompanied recitative is so-called because it uses either strings or a larger orchestra to give a much fuller sound and this results in the creation of a greater emotional tension in the linking passages. At first this form of recitative was reserved for the most intensely dramatic moments in the action, or to precede the most brilliant arias, but later its emotional charge approached that of the dramatic aria itself, for example, in Beethoven's *Fidelio* (1805).

By the end of the 19th century, distinct recitative forms were abandoned by composers such as Wagner, Debussy and Richard Strauss. In their works, the musical expression attained in the narrative passages became merged with the more lyrical 'aria' sections of the music to form a more integrated overall texture. The neo-classical operas of Stravinsky, such as *Rake's Progress* (1951), however, saw a brief revival of the old recitative *secco.*

The reading of the cards – is the highlight of Act III in Georges Bizet's popular opera, **Carmen.** *(Right, Shirley Verrett as Carmen in the Sadler's Wells Company, 1970).* **Carmen** *originally included spoken dialogue, but this was later replaced in 1875 after Bizet's death by recitative written by Ernest Guiraud.*

Reg Wilson

The male voice

There are three main categories of natural male voice: the *tenor*, the *baritone* and the *bass*. Each category has a certain range which may be subdivided further according to specific roles. Many singers are able to extend above or below these three ranges. Other less common categories include the recently revived *counter-tenor* – a high voice which covers the altro range – used increasingly in Baroque operas and roles such as Oberon in Britten's *Midsummer Night's Dream*. There is also the naturally high boy's voice, termed *treble*.

Tenor: Among the main categories, the tenor is the highest male voice and it has a long history of being the most important. This was no doubt due to its capacity for virtuosity, although its popularity was eclipsed during the heyday of the *castrati* in the 18th century. Tenors nearly always take the leading roles of the heroes in opera – a bright clear voice somehow suggesting youth and goodness. These are the lovers, the noble soldiers and the wronged suitors. Some tenors, known as *lyric tenors,* have especially light and agile voices and they are best suited for roles such as Don José in *Carmen,* and Tamino in *The Magic Flute*. The *heroic tenor,* a stronger, more powerful voice, developed along with the very dramatic operas of the 19th century.

Baritone: The middle and most common category of the male voice, the baritone appeared relatively late in operatic history. At the end of the 18th century, Mozart's wide use of it in his operas amazed the rest of Europe. Baritones usually, though not exclusively, play the villains in opera. Mozart used them in other roles, the only real villain being Don Giovanni. Others such as Figaro *(Marriage of Figaro)* and Papageno are comic roles as also in Rossini's Figaro *(Barber of Seville)* and Verdi's *Falstaff*. However, the rich dark voice of the baritone is ideally suited to conjuring up the sadism of characters like Scarpia in *Tosca,* the scheming Iago in *Otello* or the tortured tyrant of Verdi's *Macbeth*. The voice of the baritone may well describe other emotions too. Such as the warmth, maturity and wisdom which are perfectly blended in the father figure of Germont *(La Traviata)*. A few singers are able to encompass both the bass and baritone ranges. Known simply as *bass-baritones,* their rich voices are ideal for authoritarian roles such as Wotan in Wagner's *Ring*.

Bass: Resonant and deep, the bass is the lowest male voice. It was virtually non-existent in Italian opera seria, but became very important in the French Baroque operas of Lully and Rameau. The strength and nobility of the bass voice lends itself well to roles of authority and is often given to priests (Sarastro in *The Magic Flute*) or rulers (Philip II in *Don Carlos*). One of the best-known bass roles is Mussorgsky's Boris Godunov.

Tenor

Luigi Alva

A fine Peruvian tenor, Alva was born in 1927. He studied music first at Lima before going on to Milan to complete his voice training at La Scala School. He returned to Lima to make his stage début in a zarzuela (a form of Spanish opera) and followed this by playing Peppe in *Pagliacci*. Five years later he made his European début at Milan's Teatro Nuovo as Alfredo in *La Traviata* and went on to win wide acclaim as Rossini's Almaviva, showing both subtlety in his character portrayal and his great sense of comedy. After this, he sang regularly in Milan, although he also made appearances at the Metropolitan Opera and Covent Garden and several major festivals. Alva's elegant and refined style have always made him admirably suited to the works of Mozart and Rossini. He has appeared at the Aix-en-Provence, Salzburg and Glyndebourne festivals and has won great acclaim on many stages throughout the world.

Giacomo Aragall

Born in 1939, Aragall has become one of Spain's notable tenors. He studied singing in the city of his birth, Barcelona, under Francesco Puig, before going on to Italy were he completed his training under Vladimiro Badiali.

In 1963, Aragall won the Busseto singing competition which launched him in his operatic career. His début was made later the same year at La Scala in Milan, where he played the title role in Mascagni's *L'amico Fritz*. His success in Europe continued and by 1966 Aragall had made his début at London's Covent Garden as the Duke of Mantua in *Rigoletto*.

Throughout his career, Aragall has tended towards the Italian repertory, where he excels in the idiomatic phrasing of the language. The clear tone of his voice and his sensitive interpretations have made him one of the most popular tenors of his time. He has a forwardly-produced, keen-edged voice, which he uses sensitively, if not with invariably true pitch in some higher notes.

Carlo Bergonzi

Bergonzi studied in his native town under Grandini before making his début in Lecce in Rossini's *Barbiere di Seviglia,* where he took the title role of Figaro. After three years as a baritone, he left the stage for further study, this time emerging as an accomplished tenor in the title role of Giordano's *Andrea Chenier,* in 1951. Since then he has been a consistently impressive singer in a variety of roles. After his first appearance in Chicago in 1955, as Luigi in *Il tabarro,* he sang regularly at the Metropolitan Opera from 1956 to 1974, especially in roles by Verdi.

José Carreras

A Catalan Spaniard from Barcelona, Carreras was born in 1946. With Domingo, from Madrid, he is regarded as the best Spanish *tenor* since the war. Carreras studied music in his native city, making his début as Flavio in Cherubini's *Norma*.

His career advanced rapidly in the Italian repertoire, especially after meeting Monserrat Caballé, who noted his great talent and did much to further his fledgling career. By the beginning of the 1970s, he was rapidly gaining a reputation throughout Europe. By 1974 he had made his début at the New York Metropolitan and had also started recording. Since then he has broadened his repertoire; to include Mascagni, Verdi, Donizetti and Rossini. Carreras is a highly intelligent and sensitive singer with a voice of real beauty. His typical sweetness of timbre and purity of singing have made him one of the most popular lyric tenors of his generation, comparable with Bjorling.

Franco Corelli

Corelli, born in Ancona, in 1921 is one of the most outstanding *tenors* that Italy has produced. He studied in Milan, Florence and Pesaro before finally making his début in Spoleto in 1951, at the age of 30, in *Carmen*. Playing the hero, Don José, he made an impressive entry into the world of opera, where he was to excel in heroic Latin roles for the next two decades.

Well-built and handsome, Corelli also had, throughout his career, great stage charm and charisma, and always played a role for all it was worth. His Covent Garden début came in 1957, and in the mid-1950s he also started his recording career. He has made numerous records, both of complete operas and many recitals. Between 1958 and 1962 he proved himself in a string of testing roles at La Scala and from there became a regular star at the New York Metropolitan.

Now retired, Corelli had a remarkably pure voice and a deep musical intuition, which always made his interpretations both enlightening and thrilling. He possesses a large dark-coloured voice, which intensive study has enabled him to develop a strong upper registry and to vary in its tone.

James McCracken

This American *tenor* was born in Gary, Indiana, in 1926, and studied singing in New York. He made his début at the age of 27 as Rudolfo in *La Bohème,* and the following year started on a four-year stint at the New York Metropolitan, singing many supporting roles. After singing successfully in a number of European opera centres, in 1963 he returned to the Met. where he was employed as leading tenor and within 12 months embarked on a long and satisfying relationship with London's Covent Garden. He has recorded extensively, and is an exceptionally impressive performer live on stage with his large physique and dark-timbred voice. Despite this, he has tended to resist the Wagnerian roles for which he seems so fitted.

Fritz Wunderlich

Wunderlich was one of the great post-war tenors, with a beauty of tone and sensitivity to text rarely paralleled since World War II. Born in 1930, he first studied in Frieberg, later running his own dance band to finance himself. He made his début at 24 in a student production of *Die Zauberflöte,* then moved on to Stuttgart in 1955. He spent three years with the company there, building a considerable domestic reputation. By 1960 he had moved to Munich where he was to stay until his untimely death in 1966 just as he was poised to become the finest tenor of his generation.

Clive Barda

Baritone

Dietrich Fischer-Dieskau
Fischer-Dieskau, born in Berlin in 1928, is one of the most distinguished *baritones* of the 20th-century. He began his studies in Berlin but during World War II was a prisoner of war in Italy. He resumed his career in 1947 and made his concert début in Brahms' *German Requiem* at Frieburg and, the following year, made his operatic début as Posa in *Don Carlos*.

In 1949 he began regular appearances in Vienna and Munich and in 1952 he sang at the Salzburg Festival, then, in 1954–6, in the Bayreuth Festival. He first appeared in London in Delius' *A Mass of Life* under Sir Thomas Beecham, after which he made many visits to England. Two of his most notable being first performances of works by Benjamin Britten. Among his countless operatic roles his greatest include his interpretations of Count Almaviva, Don Alfonso as well as The Speaker, Barak and Mandryka. In addition to trying his hand at conducting he has become a master of lieder (songs), and has a repertory of 1000. He has recorded all Schubert's, Schumann's and Wolf's songs, most of Beethoven's, Brahms' and Strauss' and many by Mendelssohn and Liszt.

Tom Krause
Krause, a versatile and polished baritone, was born in Helsinki in 1934. He decided on an unusual career early in life and studied singing in both Vienna and Hamburg, making his début at Berlin's Staatsoper in 1959. He became a principal in Hamburg in 1962. Five years later, in 1967, he cemented an equally important relationship with the New York Metropolitan.

He has sung in a great range of operas, from Mozart's *Don Giovanni* to Krenek's *Der Goldene Bock,* and is a valuable and important member of today's international singing fraternity.

Rigoletto (baritone) finds his daughter's body.

Cornell MacNeil
Born in Minneapolis in 1922, this fine American baritone studied at the Hart College of Music in Hartford Connecticut. At the end of his training MacNeil took a series of small parts in Broadway musicals before making his operatic début in 1950, playing the part of Sorel at the première of Menotti's *The Consul* in Philadelphia. he finally became well-established however in 1959, when he substituted for indisposed singers, first at La Scala as Carlo in *Ernani* then, at the Metropolitan Opera in the title role of *Rigoletto*. MacNeil is a true Verdian baritone, with a rich tone and remarkable top register.

Hermann Prey
Born in Berlin in 1929, this outstanding *baritone* studied music in his native city making his début at the age of 23, after winning a singing competition organized by Hesse Radio Station. His first appearance on the stage in Beethoven's *Fidelio* led to his engagement, the following year in 1953, as a leading baritone with the Hamburg Staatsoper. Since then Prey has had uninterrupted success on both sides of the Atlantic. His repertoire is very wide and he has sung many of the great roles.

Ingvar Wixell
Wixell, born in the Swedish town of Lulea in 1931, is a naturally strong and resonant *baritone*. He studied in Stockholm and became established at the Opera House there in the mid-1950s, after making his début as Papageno. He has retained his connection ever since. As his fame spread abroad in the 1960s, offers of work took him away with ever more frequency and he made his début in Chicago, San Francisco and Covent Garden during these years.

Bass-baritone

Donald McIntyre
McIntyre was born in Auckland, New Zealand, in 1934, and went to Guildhall School of Music in London during the 1950s to further his studies and prepare himself for a career in opera. His naturally rich and resonant voice in the *bass-baritone* register soon attracted attention, and he made his début in 1959 with the Welsh National Opera in Verdi's *Nabucco*. This led to his engagement at Sadler's Wells for seven years, starting in 1960.

By 1967 he was ready to move on, and in the following year he made his début at both Covent Garden and at Bayreuth. He has remained a regular at both ever since, while also a guest at Hamburg and Milan. He is one of a group of singers who established British singers internationally in the late 1960s.

Bass

Kurt Böhme
Böhme, born in Dresden in 1908, studied music at the Dresden Conservatory with Karl Kluge, and made his début in his native city in 1930, at the age of 22. As his voice matured, he became increasingly a mainstay of the company at Dresden, where he remained until 1950. It was this loyalty to a single company which restricted his interntational reputation. However, in the 1950s he travelled to Britain and the US, appearing in operas at Covent Garden and the New York Metropolitan, where he earned warm praise.

Böhme has also travelled very successfully to South America. Today he lives in retirement in Germany. A heroic *bass* with a big, rich tone, his interpretations were consistently interesting and rewarding both on stage and on record. His most famous role was Baron Ochs (in *Der Rosenkavalier*) which he first sang in 1942 and in which his rich voice and sense of humour had full play.

Nicholai Ghiaurov
One of this century's great *basses,* Ghiaurov was born in 1929 in Lydjene near Velingrad, Bulgaria. He studied first in Sofia where in 1949 he gained sufficient accolades to allow him to continue his training in Leningrad. After a glowing apprenticeship in Moscow, he made his début there in 1955 as Don Basilio in Mozart's *The Marriage of Figaro*. After returning to Sofia the following year, he quickly moved on to opera stages all through the continent. Within the next six years he played all the great bass roles in opera, including Boris, Mephistopheles, and Padre Guardino. The 1962 season was a particularly active one for him – seeing his first appearances both at Covent Garden and in Vienna, where he has sung regularly ever since.

Ghiaurov has a splendid voice and a quick musical intelligence, which comes across especially well on record. His ability to evoke character through telling interpretations and vocal subtleties is second to none, and his impressive stage presence is attested to by all who have seen him.

The female voice

There are three main categories of female voice in opera – the *soprano,* the *mezzo-soprano* and the *contralto.* The range and quality of each category may vary and further sub-divisions may be made according to the requirements of particular roles.

Soprano: The highest category of female voice, the term derives from the Italian *sopra* meaning 'above'. Traditionally, the soprano plays opposite the tenor as the heroine in opera, although this has only been the case since the decline of the castrati in the mid-18th century – they had previously taken the lead roles within the high voice range.

In the second half of the 18th century, composers began to recognise the potential of different voice qualities within the soprano range. Mozart created a great variety of soprano roles, among them his Queen of the Night, written for famous coloratura singer, Josefa Weber Hofer.

Roles for 19th century coloratura sopranos became particularly elaborate with Rossini, Bellini and Donizetti. As the century progressed, volume rather than agility became the desired quality. Concert halls and orchestras increased in size and Wagner and Verdi required greater intensity and tone control for their *dramatic soprano* roles.

The voice of the *lyric soprano,* however, is warmer and gentler in tone and conveys great emotion rather than drama. Lyric sopranos usually take the roles of the young or the vulnerable, such as Mimi *(La Bohème)* and Violetta *(Traviata).* The *soprano lyrico spinto,* however, is more vigorous and a typical role is Desdemona.

Mezzo-soprano: Literally 'half-soprano', this is the middle range of the female voice. The mezzo had a darker, thicker and lower voice than the soprano, although the roles for mezzo-sopranos only began to emerge in opera in the second half of the 18th century, as composers sought more variety in female singing. Mezzos usually play the supporting roles to the heroine, such as the nurse or confidante – Suzuki *(Butterfly)* and Emilia *(Otello),* for instance – or the mature married woman or rival, such as Kate Pinkerton *(Butterfly)* or Herodias *(Salome).* Two lead roles for mezzos are Carmen and Delilah.

Contralto: Derived from the words *contra* (against) and *alto* (high) the term contralto refers to the lowest and least common of the female voice categories – few roles for contraltos appear in opera. Popular in the 17th century for comic parts, the deeper register of the contralto voice has always made it suitable for mature roles – matronly mothers, queens and so forth. In the 18th century their dramatic potential was more fully recognized, the most famous lead contralto role being the part of Orfeo in Gluck's *Orfeo ed Euridice.*

Soprano

Inge Borkh

Swiss *soprano* Inge Borkh, was born in 1921. She studied acting at the Max Reinhart Seminary in Vienna and began a career as an actress before discovering a natural ability for singing. After completing voice training in Vienna and Milan she took her first major operatic role in 1951, appearing as Magda in *The Consul,* at Basle.

She made her American début in San Francisco in 1952, in the title role of *Elektra* which, along with her Lady Macbeth, has remained one of her most successful parts. Borkh is also one of the leading interpreters of Turandot. She is capable of great dramatic expression in very demanding roles.

Monserrat Caballé

Spanish *soprano,* Monserrat Caballé, was born in 1933. After thorough training in Barcelona, she made her début in Basel in 1956. She remained there in repertory until 1959 then moved to Bremen for three years. By this time, her impressive range of roles included operas by Richard Strauss, Prokofiev and Wagner as well as Verdi and Donizetti. Since the mid 1970s she has been one of the world's leading sopranos.

Mirella Freni

Freni, born in Modena, Italy, in 1935, has been one of the truly great Puccinian and Mozartian *sopranos* of her time. She studied in her home town, where she made her début as Micaela in *Carmen* in 1955. She quickly gained work throughout Italy in the provinces, but her international fame really came about in 1960 after her appearances as Zerlina at the Glyndebourne production of *Don Giovanni.* Soon she was established throughout Europe and in demand from every leading conductor, opera house and recording company to sing in such roles as Mimi in *La Bohème,* Elvira in *I Puritani,* and Marguerite in *Faust.* Freni is noted for her lightness of touch and charming acting.

Gundula Janowitz

Born in Berlin in 1937, Janowitz is a fine lyric *soprano* with a rich, creamy tone and a large range. She studied singing in Graz, making her début at the Vienna Opera in 1960, before taking on Wagnerian roles at Bayreuth for the next two years. By the early 1970s she had become regarded as one of the best interpreters of Strauss and Wagner as well as being a fine Mozartian, which demonstrates the extent of her repertoire.

Gwyneth Jones

Born in Pontnewynydd, Wales, in 1936, Gwyneth Jones has established herself as one of the outstanding British *sopranos* of the post-war years, capable of singing both the lighter and the most demanding roles.

She trained at the Royal College of Music in London with Ruth Packer and Arnold Smith before moving to Siena and Geneva to complete her studies. She remained in Europe to make her début, in Zurich in 1962, in Gluck's masterpiece, *Orfeo ed Euridice.* She played Orfeo. After this, events moved quickly in her career, and she made her début at Covent Garden the following

season. By the mid-1960s she had appeared in both Vienna and Bayreuth, and was well on her way to a top-flight career. Several record companies showed interest in her, and she has since recorded for, among others, Decca, Deutsche Grammophon and Philips, either in recital or as part of a complete opera cast. She has an unusually big repertoire, excelling in Wagner and Richard Strauss as well as Cherubini and Verdi.

Evelyn Lear

Born in Brooklyn, New York, in January 1928, Lear is one of a handful of American sopranos to establish herself successfully in Europe. She studied at the New York Juilliard School of Music in New York, making her debut in Berlin in 1958, taking the part of The Composer in Strauss' *Ariadne.* In 1962 her great success in the title part in Berg's *Lulu,* at the Vienna Festival, brought her instant fame and world-wide recognition.

Pilar Lorengar

Born in Saragossa, Spain, in 1928, Lorengar has become a *soprano* with a great deal of tonal and interpretive beauty. She studied singing in Madrid, and made her début in the same city in 1949. At this stage of her career she had been trained as, and had sung as, a mezzo-soprano. This was to continue for another two years before, in 1951, she converted to full soprano. By the middle of the 1950s she had made her full operatic début as a soprano, singing among other roles Cherubino *(Figaro)* and Violetta *(La Traviata).*

Lorengar has spent most of her career within the Mozart, Puccini and Verdi repertoire, where the clarity and lightness of her fine voice are most favourably displayed. When she has moved to more dramatic music, it is invariably the lighter roles which she plays and with her rather placid temperament, she is especially suited to the roles of classical heroines. Since the late 1960s she has made a number of operatic and recital records for Decca.

Jessye Norman

Born in 1945 in Georgia USA, Jessye Norman is one of the few black divas to attain world fame. She studied in Washington DC, Maryland and then at the University of Michigan in Ann Arbor, but it was not until winning first prize in Munich at the Bavarian Radio Corporation's International Music Competition that her singing career really got under way. In 1965 she made her début in Berlin in the demanding role of *Tannhäuser's* Elisabeth. She was very quickly sought after by other opera houses, and record companies, who were impressed by her richness of voice and commanding personal presence.

In 1982 she won the American 'Musician of the Year' award, and in the same year, was awarded an honorary Doctorate of Music from Howard University and Boston Conservatory. In 1984 she won her greatest honour when she was invested by the French government as 'Commandeur de L'Ordre des Arts et des Lettres.'

Jessye Norman with Sir Colin Davis (right).

Katia Ricciarelli
Born in 1946 in Rovigo, Northern Italy, Ricciarelli has become one of the pre-eminent *sopranos* of the past ten years. After studying in Venice, she made her début as Mimi in 1969.

Her initial reputation was made with Verdi, although she also showed an early affinity for Donizetti. By her Covent Garden début in 1974, however, she was also both an accomplished Puccinian and outstanding in Gluck, and to date, she has sung and recorded most of Puccini heroines and is a favourite singer of Von Karajan.

Irmgard Seefried
Born in Köngetried, Germany, in 1919, Seefried was an outstanding *soprano*. Her vocal talent was recognized at an early age and she studied music and singing at both Augsburg and Munich. The outbreak of the Second World War delayed her stage début but after meeting Richard Strauss in Aachen, where she spent most of the war years, she was invited by him to sing the role of The Composer in *Ariadne,* for his 80th birthday celebrations in 1944.

During the 1950s she became one of the great international stars, making her first appearance at the New York Metropolitan in 1955 and also doing regular performances at Salzburg.

By the late 1960s, Seefried's career was entering its 'Indian summer', and the richness of tone and flexibility of range and timbre was beginning to wane. She decided to withdraw from public performance, leaving her reputation intact as one of the greatest sopranos of our time. Her recordings have sold throughout the world.

Dame Joan Sutherland
Dame Joan has had a long and extraordinarily successful career. Born in Sydney, Australia, in 1926, her early musical training took place in that city. Her exceptional talent was quickly realized and admission to the Royal College of Music in London was arranged, where she studied under Clive Carey. She made her Covent Garden début in 1952, in a production of the *Magic Flute* at the age of 25 and quickly established herself as a dazzling new coloratura *soprano* with a virtually limitless

potential in lyric opera.

Soon after this, a string of phenomenally successful records for Decca made her the equal in popularity to such greats as Callas and Schwartzkopf. Her vast success spread to the USA after her Metropolitan début in 1961 and during the 1970s and 1980s she has helped establish Sydney Opera House on the international circuit. Her voice is famed for its richness and range.

Rita Streich
Streich was one of the extraordinary wave of German *sopranos* to emerge directly after the Second World War. Born in 1920 in Barnaul, of German and Russian parentage, she studied singing in both Augsburg and Berlin during the 1930s.

After the war she joined the Berlin State Opera, where she stayed for five years. By 1950, her reputation was assured and during the early part of the next decade, she made appearances in all the major European opera houses and also began a distinguished recording career.

The 1960s saw Streich at the height of her fame, during which time she made recital recordings that are still prized.

Mezzo-soprano

Teresa Berganza
Berganza, born in Madrid in 1935, has become Spain's outstanding post-war *mezzo-soprano*. She studied singing as a teenager in Madrid under Lola Rodrigues Aragon and made her début as Dorabella in Mozart's *Cosi fan Tutte,* at the prestigious Aix-En-Provence Festival. Her success there led to immediate offers of roles at La Scala in Milan, and then, in 1958 she played Cherubino in the Glyndebourne production of *Le Nozze di Figaro.*

Thus her career took off from a firm Mozartian footing, and it was as a Mozartian that she made some of her early recital records. Within a few years, she had branched out into performances of Rossini and other early 19th century composers, and had also begun to acquire a reputation as

The mezzo-soprano, Teresa Berganza (below).

a singer of Spanish song. During the 1960s, her career flourished in the USA and she recorded extensively for a number of record companies while still appearing in operas.

Fiorenza Cossotto
Cossotto, born in Crescentino in 1935, has had a distinguished career in Italy as a *mezzo-soprano*. She studied singing in Turin for a number of years before coming to Milan's La Scala in 1957 to make her début as Mathilde in Poulenc's *Dialogues des Carmelites.* By 1961 she was ready to appear in London as Leonora in Donizetti's *La Favorita* at Covent Garden and within a few years she was also established at the Metropolitan in New York, settled into a clearly delineated Italian opera repertoire.

Marilyn Horne
Marilyn Horne is one of the very few American singers to progress to the front rank in opera since World War II. Her break into the profession came in an unorthodox way when, in 1954, at the age of 25, she landed the job of ghosting the vocals for Dorothy Dandridge in the Hollywood film, *Carmen Jones.* This led to other work in the U.S.A. and by 1957 Horne had moved to Germany and made her European début in Gelsenkirchen in the role of Giulietta in Offenbach's *Tales of Hoffman.*

Horne has been a favourite at the New York Metropolitan Opera since 1970, and is currently one of the strongest, most flexible *mezzo-sopranos* in the world. Since first singing with Joan Sutherland in 1962 in a New York production of *Beatrice di Tenda,* they have been friends and colleagues.

Contralto

Janet Baker
Born in 1933 in Hatfield, Yorkshire, the mezzo-soprano and contralto Janet Baker first sang in local choirs. She then studied in London under Helen Isepp and won second prize in the Kathleen Ferrier Award for 1956. In the same year she joined the Glyndebourne Chorus and soon began to appear in pre-classical operas – Gluck's Orpheus in 1958 and as the Sorceress in *Dido and Aeneas.* In 1963 she was Polly in Britten's version of *The Beggar's Opera* and has since sung in other of his operas. Her USA debut was at Town Hall, New York, in 1966 and she has since given many varied recitals in Britain and around the world.

Helen Watts
Born in Milford Haven, Wales in 1927, Helen Watts was at first undecided as to her vocation. After studying at the Royal Academy of Music, she proceeded to train and develop her natural contralto into a powerful and versatile voice. She joined the BBC chorus at first but then took the lead role in a broadcast of Gluck's *Orpheus and Eurydice.* After this highly succesful debut, she soon became considered one of the leading oratorio singers in Britain. Her fame became worldwide in the 1960s, following roles in Handel's operas and parts in both Wagner and Britten productions. She has also sung Brahms and Schoenberg *lieder*.

The prima donna

Prima donna, Italian for 'first lady', is an operatic term which has developed from being a simple technical phrase, to one charged with meaning. When it was first used in the mid-17th century, it referred simply to the singer – soprano or mezzo – who sang the most arias in an opera. Later, the phrase was used to describe operatic stars of great vocal ability who also possessed a certain type of personality – tempestuous, over sensitive, hard to please, jealous of other leading ladies and often difficult to work with. This meaning of the term has slipped into general use outside the operatic world.

One of the earliest recorded prima donnas was an English singer, Catherine Tofts of the Drury Lane Theatre, in the early 18th century. Famous for her tempestuous relationship with her managers, and for her florid embellishment of her roles, people flocked from miles around to see her perform, rather than to watch the particular opera as a whole.

The first prima donnas to rise to international fame, even in the face of fierce competition from the ambitious castrati, were two Italian ladies, soprano, Francesca Cuzzoni and the mezzo singer, 'Faustina' Bordoni. The personal antagonism between these two contemporary stars, singing in both London and Venice in the 1720s, meant that rivalry and feuding soon became another widely accepted characteristic of the prima donna.

The phenomenon of the prima donna had a significant influence on composers of opera. Mozart, for example, began a practice that was to continue for many years – that of composing specially with the voice and ability of a particular prima donna in mind.

The leading singer of Mozart's day was Catalina Cavalieri, for whom he wrote the operas *Die Entführung* (1791) and *Der Schauspiel-direktor* (1786). The more difficult arias in these were reserved for her, being specifically intended to show off the versatility of her voice. Special arias for her to sing were also inserted in *Don Giovanni* (1787).

By the 19th century, the golden age of bel canto, performances given by prima donnas had a new dramatic intensity. During the years when Gioachino Rossini, Vicenzo Bellini and Gaetano Donizetti were composing, there emerged some female star personalities who were much larger than life than, perhaps, any of today's leading singers. With two singers, more than any other, the term Prima donna became almost synonymous – Giuditta Pasta and Maria Malibran.

Pasta dominated the opera world for ten years. She had an exciting and very dramatic voice which demonstrated just how great human vocal range and power could be. She inspired Bellini's *Sonnambula* (1831), *Norma* (1831) and

The soprano, Maria Callas (above) who recreated many of the roles played by the famous 19th-century prima donnas, Giuditta Pasta and Maria Malibran.

Beatrice di Tenda (1833) as well as Donizetti's *Anna Bolena* (1830). Malibran, who created the title role of Donizetti's *Maria Stuarda* (1835), brought even greater dramatic excitement to her performances and was a more accurate singer than Pasta. She had a short but legendary career, and a tempestuous personal life. Tragically, she died young, aged 28, but left an important legacy in her definitive examples of the enormous emotional possibilities of great romantic opera.

After Pasta and Malibran, a number of other great Prima donnas followed in the 19th century – Patti, Melba, Lilli Lehman. In the 20th century, Maria Callas recreated many of Pasta's and Malibrans's former roles. Today, the term is more sparingly used in the opera world, as few modern singers reach the level of fame of the great personalities of the past.

Ballet in opera

Ballet first became an important element in opera during the 17th century in France, and although it has appeared in various forms in opera throughout history, it is with the French operatic tradition that it has always been most strongly associated.

When opera first arrived in France from Italy under Louis XIV, the French *ballet de cour* (court ballet) was already well-established as the favourite form of entertainment. Consequently, ballet had to be introduced into the first Italian operas performed there in order to accommodate French tastes. As French operas found their own direction with the compositions of Lully and Rameau, almost every act had a ballet scene. At the climax of these works,

the King himself often appeared and danced a few steps, thus guaranteeing ballet's popularity.

The use of dance in Italian opera, however, was not unknown. Its first use had been as early as Caccini's *Euridice* (1600) and Monteverdi's *Orfeo* (1607), both of which end in a short dance scene, and it continued to be used in some 17th century operas.

Dance was not always an acceptable part of opera though – in the Vienna of Mozart's time, the Emperor Joseph II decided to ban it and Mozart had to fight for the retention of the ballet scenes in his *Marriage of Figaro* and *Don Giovanni.* To Mozart, ballet was no mere diversionary entertainment, but an integral part of the plots. Weber, in the 19th century, took the use of ballet a stage further in his opera *Silvana* and had a silent heroine who danced while others sang.

Meanwhile, at the Paris Opéra, ballet continued to have a prominent position and in the 18th century a form known as *opéra-ballet* (an equal mixture of the two) had become popular. Then in the 19th century the large scale Grand Operas usually included a ballet scene – especially after Meyerbeer's brilliant use of it in the 1831 opera *Robert le Diable.*

It soon became customary for ballet scenes to be set at the opening of the second act of operas, so that late arrivals to performances, who preferred to dine first, would not miss their favourite part. Ballet was so important to French audiences that visiting composers to Paris were obliged to include special ballet scenes, for instance, Rossini's *William Tell,* Donizetti's *La Favorita,* and Verdi's *I Lombardi, Il Trovatore, Don Carlos* and *Otello.*

Verdi, however, resisted pressure to include one in *Rigoletto.* Wagner also had to insert a ballet scene into his *Tannhäuser,* before it could be performed in Paris, but he flouted tradition by setting it at the opening of the opera. 'Added' ballets were usually referred to as *divertissements,* as they invariably added nothing to the plot.

Apart from Paris, the other centre of 19th century ballet was Russia. Tchaikovsky incorporated a ballet scene into most of his operas, such as *Eugene Onegin* and *The Queen of Spades.* In addition, the ballet music from Borodin's *Prince Igor* has become popular – *The Polovtsian Dances.*

In 20th century opera, ballet is still very much in evidence. Sopranos have to cope with the evocative and sensual *Dance of the Seven Veils* if they wish to play the title role of Richard Strauss's *Salome.* Then there is the orgy before the Golden Calf in Schönberg's *Moses and Aaron.* Alban Berg also has a dance sequence in his *Wozzeck.*

Tippet's *Midsummer Marriage,* has produced another popular piece, often played separately – the *Ritual Dances.* Britten also uses ballet in his *Gloriana* and *Death in Venice.*

A Listener's Guide

Bizet

Carmen
Despite its poor intial reception in Paris in 1875, Bizet's last and greatest opera soon became one of the most popular ever, thanks to its dramatic brilliance. Set in Seville in 1820, Carmen, a gypsy, bewitches Don José, a corporal of the guard. When she is arrested in a fight, Carmen persuades him to release her. After being imprisoned in his turn for this, Don José follows her, fights with his captain over her and then flees with her and a group of smugglers into the mountains. This life, however, does not suit Don José, and Carmen, who has fallen for the bullfighter Escamillo, rejects him. Back in Seville, she promises herself to Escamillo before the bullfight, but José confronts her outside the bullring and stabs her fatally. From a trite novel by Mérimée, Bizet created a masterpiece – the German philosopher Nietzsche claimed it greater than Wagner.

L'arlesienna (Suites 1 & 2)
Bizet wrote the incidental music to this play, written by Alphonse Daudet, in a terrific hurry trying to meet a commission from the playwright. What emerged was a deal of orchestral music which rivals anything else he wrote for the splendour of its melodies, harmonies and rhythms. Today most often played simply as two orchestral suites, it is repeatedly given at concerts and laid down on records, being a favourite of both performers and the public.

Les Pêcheurs De Perles (The Pearl Fishers)
The opera has an exotic setting, being placed in Ceylon in a remote period, and the music has occasional exotic references: however, the plot is a tried-and-true blood, gore and love mixture to be found in so many operas of the last century, and it is here that the work's major weakness lies. The Pearl Fishers is a relatively early work of Bizet's, having its permière in 1863, a full twelve years before Carmen. Still, there are some truly remarkable musical passages in the work, none more so than the first-act duet 'Au fond du temple saint', which is even now often recorded or performed in singers' recitals. Many of the choral passages are also of the highest inspiration, and are quite worthy of the author of Carmen. In fact, it anticipates that masterpiece both in its exotic setting and in its sensual lyricism.

Djamileh
This one-act opera, Carmen's immediate predecessor, has an exotic theme. Based in Turkey at some indeterminate ancient time, it tells the story of a slave who finds her master has tired of her and finally succeeds in winning back his love. The work, though no great success with the public of the time, is a brilliant early example of Bizet applying the musical rules to opera which would bring about his masterpiece in Carmen three years later. The vibrancy of the music, the realism of the characterisations, and the strong, clear colours in the orchestra and vocal lines make it a compelling work.

Donizetti

Don Pasquale
Donizetti's greatest opera was first performed in Paris in 1843, using a libretto by Ruffini and himself. It was an instant success. In the opera, Don Pasquale, an elderly bachelor, wants to marry to deny his nephew, Ernesto, his fortune because he disapproves of his choice of bride, Norina. The young couple arrange for Pasquale to offer his hand to "Sofronia" (Norina in disguise) who then behaves so badly that Pasquale begs Ernesto to marry her instead.

Lucia di Lammermoor
Premièred at Naples in 1835, with a libretto by Cammarano (based on Scott's novel *The Bride of Lammermoor*), this has become Donizetti's most popular opera. Lucy Ashton (Lucia) loves Edgar Ravenswood, a family enemy. She is shown a forged letter, supposedly written by Edgar, and so marries Lord Bucklaw. The wedding ceremony is interrupted by Edgar who curses Lucy for her betrayal. Lucy then goes mad with grief, kills her new husband and dies herself. Edgar, in remorse, commits suicide.

Gounod

Faust
One of the most successful operas ever written, *Faust* received its première in Paris in 1859. It is based on the poem by Goethe, with a libretto by Barbier and Carré, though it lacks Goethe's grandeur. Faust, a scholar, makes a bargain with Méphistophélès: in return for eternal youth and the beautiful Marguerite, he promises his soul. Having ruined Marguerite, Faust deserts here. Her brother Valentine, returning from the wars, challenges Faust to a duel and is killed. Marguerite, in prison for killing her baby, is condemned to death but still refuses to escape with Faust. As she dies, heaven opens to receive her with angelic choruses. Méphistophélès then appears to drag Faust down to Hell as promised. Despite its sentimentality, Gounod's version of *Faust* proved very popular even in Germany, where one critic thought that Gounod could not be French!

Mireille
Written between the more famous and larger scale *Faust* and *Romeo et Juliette*, Gounod's *Mireille* is a refreshingly simple and lyrical work. Set in the town of Arles, the story revolves round the passions, amorous and otherwise, of a close-knit community in which the young and beautiful Mireille plays a central role. Gounod based the work on a poem by the Provençal poet Mistral, and the music, which incorporates ancient and medieval songs, very much captures the charm of its setting. Therefore, despite Gounod's frequent tendency to over-heighten some of the opera's most dramatic scenes, *Mireille* which ends happily (a revision of the original ending) is a diverting musical work, and rewarding listening.

Romeo et Juliette
Inspired by Shakespeare's play and adapted by Gounod's regular librettists Barbier and Carré, *Romeo et Juliette* was the composer's second huge success. It was an instant hit when first shown at the Paris Théâtre-Lyrique in 1867, and its tunefulness and drama has kept it constantly in the French repertoire (even if it is less frequently seen abroad).

The opera has the same musical grandeur and dramatic scope associated with *Faust,* and this gives both leads ample opportunity to sing a stream of beautiful lyrical melodies. The only criticism must be that it is at times excessively theatrical but the melodrama, though never far away, is kept under control, especially in the touching last act.

Lehar

The Merry Widow
One of the most popular of all Viennese operettas, with a libretto by Viktor Leon and Leo Stein, this was first performed in Vienna in 1905. Although no great success at first, its fame soon spread round the world; it has been translated into 25 languages. The light-hearted plot revolves around the attempts of Baron Mirko Zeta to obtain the immense fortune of the Merry Widow, Hanna Glawari, for his impoverished country, Pontevedria, by getting his young compatriot, Danilo, to marry her. Its bubbling gaiety and romantic setting have made it lastingly popular. It was Adolf Hitler's favourite opera.

Das Land des Lachelns
In this work, better known in Britain as *The Land of Smiles,* Lehár wrote the perfect operatic vehicle for his close friend Richard Tauber, the pre-eminent tenor of the period. There is a genuine philosophy of kindness and self-sacrifice behind the thin plot, and the music, rich in memorable melodies and subtle rhythmic variations, has a great deal to savour, despite a rather banal sentimentality.

Frederica
Lehár always aspired to the writing of what he saw as 'serious' opera. *Frederica* is a well-balanced and wholly charming opera, which combines a serious storyline with immediately attractive music.

Leoncavallo

I Pagliacci
First performed in Milan in 1892, with a text by Leoncavallo himself, *Pagliacci* (*Clowns*) is based on a real event. Canio, head of a troupe of actors, warns his wife Nedda against infidelity. She then repulses the advances of Tonio, another actor, but Tonio hears her and her lover Silvio plotting, and tells Canio who stabs his wife during the clown play.

Mascagni

Cavalleria Rusticana
This one-act opera, with a libretto by Menasci and Targioni-Tozzetti, was first performed in Rome in 1890, where it was an immediate success – indeed it was Mascagni's only real success. Turiddu, a Sicilian villager, in theory in love with Santuzza, is still fond of Lola, now Alfio's wife. Informed of this, Alfio kills Turiddu in a duel – showing 'rustic chivalry'.

Puccini

Turandot
Completed after Puccini's death in 1925 by Alfano, *Turandot* was first performed under Toscanini in Milan in 1926. The libretto was written by Adami and Simoni after the 1761 play by Carlo Gozzi. The cruel Princess of China, Turandot, poses three riddles for each of her suitors to answer – if they fail, they are executed. The unknown Prince Calaf, son of the deposed King of Tartary, accepts and passes the test. He then challenges the princess to discover his name by morning. This she attempts to do by torturing a Tartar slave girl, Liu. But, rather than reveal it, Liu kills herself. Calaf then himself discloses it and Turandot realizes she loves him.

La Bohème
Puccini's great opera of bohemian life in four acts, was written to a libretto by Giuseppe Giacosa and Luigi Illica. It took time to establish itself as one of his 'big three' successes – audiences were not used to seeing depictions of such low life. The story is set in Paris' Latin Quarter, where four bohemians share a garret. The poet Rodolfo meets their neighbour Mimi and they fall in love, while the painter Marcello regains his old lover Musetta. But both relationships became strained and they part. Finally, Rodolfo and Mimi are reunited when Mimi, ill with consumption, is brought back to the studio, there to die.

Madame Butterfly
Despite a disastrous first night in Milan in 1904, *Madame Butterfly* soon became one of Puccini's most successful operas after some small revision. Based on a drama by David Belasco, itself probably derived from a true story, it marks the highpoint of Puccini's Italian lyricism, mingled with Far Eastern colouring. Lieutenant Pinkerton, a United States naval officer stationed in Japan, marries a Japanese geisha girl, known as Butterfly, Pinkerton returns to America; Butterfly bears his child and waits for his return, comforted by Sharpless, the U.S. consul. Pinkerton returns with his new American wife and demands his son. Grief-stricken, Butterfly hands him over and then commits suicide.

Mozart

The Marriage of Figaro
The first collaboration between Mozart and da Ponte, *Figaro* was based on the notorious play by Beaumarchais and first performed in Vienna in 1786. Although the plot is highly artificial, Mozart's music brings all his characters vividly to life. Figaro is to marry Susanna but the Count also has his eye on her. The plot deals with Figaro's thwarting of the Count, complicated by the behaviour of the page Cherubino, who imagines himself in love with every woman he meets, including the Countess. The Countess, tired of her husband's infidelities, impersonates Susanna and meets the Count in the garden. Finally, all is revealed and forgiven.

The Magic Flute
First performed in Vienna in September 1791 Mozart's *singspiel* combined allegory, fantasy and pantomime to win great popular acclaim in Vienna. It also concealed Masonic references among some of Mozart's most exquisite music (Mozart was himself a freemason). Set in a fairytale world, the often comic plot takes the heroic Prince Tamino, with the most unheroic Papageno, from the realm of the Queen of Night – a sinister figure – to the Temple of the Sun, ruled by an omniscient High Priest, Sarastro. Through various ordeals, all characters find their appropriate fate.

Don Giovanni
The second great opera Mozart composed with da Ponte, Don Giovanni had its première in Prague in 1787. The Don Juan legend was treated as a comic drama, undershot with melancholy. It opens with the Don being pursued by Donna Anna – one of his more difficult conquests. In the ensuing scuffle he kills her father, the Commander. Then follows a series of thwarted seductions, punctuated by quarrels, until the Don invites the statue of the Commander to supper. It accepts – to take him to hell.

Cosi fan tutte
Also called *The School for Lovers, Cosi fan tutte* was Mozart's last *opera buffa*, first performed in Vienna in 1790. Thought immoral in the 19th century, it is now considered a sublime human comedy. In it, two officers accept a wager that their respective lovers will resist all temptations in their absence. The officers take tearful leave of their ladies to return in disguise, and finally to undermine their lovers' loyalties. The men then resume their true guises to pretend fury, before all are reconciled at the end.

Die Entführung aus dem Serail
This opera, often known simply as the *Seraglio,* is a classic example of comic *opera buffa*. It has a lively story, a light subject and a happy ending in its tale of two virtuous European girls and their travails at the hands of a Turkish Sultan in his harem. It is an opera full of gaiety and tremendous vitality, and the musical writing is wonderfully lyrical. Written by Mozart when he was 26, in 1782, it is a fully mature work, packed with drama but one with the lightest of touches. Mozart paints his character portraits extremely swiftly here, and this makes the work really come alive.

La Clemenza di Tito
Mozart's last *opera seria* and one of his 'big seven', with a text by Metastasio altered by Mazzolà, *Tito* was first performed in Prague in 1791. Its highly complex plot concerns the varying marital ambitions of the Emperor Titus that anger Vitellia, who plans a conspiracy. This is both discovered and forgiven by Titus. This most unusual plot was dictated by political events – the French Revolution was raging – and Mozart wanted to show a wise, forgiving ruler. The opera was long damned for its rigid coldness but is now better liked.

Lucio Silla
A story of life and love in Ancient Rome, *Silla,* an opera seria in three acts, is one of Mozart's youthful works. It is comparable in form and style to this other early works *Ascanio in Alba* and *La Finta Giardiniera*. All these operas show the astonishing mastery which the composer, still in his teens, already had over the operatic form. However, some may be put off by the conventionality of the libretto and the relative conservatism of the music – which show the composer content, at this stage, to work within contemporary boundaries of operatic form. But it would be a mistake to dismiss Mozart's *Lucio Silla* and other of his early works on this score, as they are full of youthful charm and zest.

Idomeneo
First performed in Munich in 1781, with a libretto by Varesco, *Idomeneo* was Mozart's first major work for stage and perhaps the greatest *opera seria* ever written. Idomeneo, king of Crete, returning from the Trojan War, vows that if he survives a storm he will sacrifice to Poseidon the first creature he sees on shore. To his horror, this turns out to be his son, Idamante. He urges Idamante to flee with Electra to Argos. Electra, who loves Idamante, agrees but Idamante secretly loves Ilia, a Trojan captive. The impatient Poseidon sends a storm and a monster to ravage Crete. Idamante kills the monster, but Ilia offers herself in his place. Poseidon then relents, Idomeneo abdicates and Idamante succeeds him.

Tosca

Based on the very popular play by Sardou, with a libretto by Giacosa and Illica, *Tosca* was first performed in Rome in 1900. Cavaradossi, a republican painter, helps Angelotti, an escaped political prisoner, to escape from a church. Scarpia, the cruel, lecherous police chief, arrives and has Cavaradossi arrested and tortured. Scarpia, who lusts after Tosca, a famous singer and Cavaradossi's mistress, promises Tosca her lover's liberty if she gives herself to him. Tosca pretends to consent and Scarpia signs a mock execution order. Tosca then seizes a knife, stabs him and goes to tell her lover of the fake execution he must endure. The shots ring out but Cavaradossi falls dead. Scarpia has tricked Tosca. As the police attempt to arrest her, she climbs the prison wall and throws herself to her death.

Manon Lescaut

Based on Prevost's novel, it was first performed in Turin in 1893. Des Grieux falls in love with the young Manon, and they elope. But Manon deserts Des Grieux and goes to live with an elderly roué, Géronte. Then Des Grieux reappears to revive her love. Géronte has her deported as a prostitute but Des Grieux follows her to Louisiana, where she dies in his arms, reuinited in a desert outside New Orleans.

La Fanciulla del West

With a libretto by Civinini and Zangarini after Belasco's drama *The Girl of the Golden West,* this was first performed in New York in 1910. Set in California during the Gold Rush, its heroine Minnie falls in love with an outlaw, Johnson, hiding him in her cabin. When he is discovered by the sheriff, she plays cards for his life and wins by cheating. But Johnson is still captured and is only saved from hanging by Minnie riding up to plead for his life. Together they start a new life. The first performance was conducted by Toscanini, but was not initially very popular. It has since become very popular.

Il Tabarro

Puccini's one-act opera about low-life love and death on the barges of the Seine is an arresting work. Based only on a simple story-line, it shows devastating psychological insights into the main characters, and Puccini's uncanny ability to evoke a whole picture and mood through his orchestral introductions and accompaniments to the action. This short work though somewhat neglected, is one of this century's greatest operas, and perhaps its author's most flawless.

Le Villi

Puccini's first opera, *Le Villi*, is a short, one-act work. Based on a folk tale with a similar storyline to Adam's ballet *Giselle,* the work at times suffers from a ridiculous libretto. The music, however, clearly shows Puccini's melodic and dramatic gifts, and the characteristic Puccinian energy comes through in the rhythmic vitality of the score.

La Rondine

Set in Paris and Nice during the Second Empire this attempt at a sort of Italian operetta was doomed from the start due to internal and external inconsistencies. However, there is much to savour in terms of pure music, and in Puccini's unfailing good musical taste. Apart from some weaknesses of story and characterization, the opera can be enjoyed for its refined writing and its elegant, captivating melodies.

Rossini

Il Barbiere de Siviglia

Despite a fiasco of a première in Rome in 1816, *The Barber of Seville* – its libretto by Sterbini founded on Beaumarchais' play of 30 years earlier – has become Rossini's most successful opera. Set in 17th century Spain, it tells how Count Almaviva loves Rosina, the ward of Dr Bartolo, who wants to marry her himself. Almaviva poses as Linoro, a poor student, and enlists the aid of the wily Figaro, a barber, with entry to the household. He helps the young lovers to thwart successfully all the old man's varied plots and finally to elope together. Another *Barber of Seville* had been written by Paisiello in 1782, which made Rossini first call his *Almaviva ossia L'inutile Precauzione.*

L'Italiana in Algeri

First performed in 1813 in Venice, this was Rossini's first major comic opera, written in just over three weeks with a libretto by Anelli. The 'Italiana' is Isabella, who is looking for her lover, Lindoro, a slave of the Bey of Algiers. The Bey falls in love with her too, but the lovers are finally reunited. The opera is exuberant, despite a weak plot.

La Cenerentola

First performed in Rome in 1817 with a libretto by Ferretti, the plot follows Perrault's well-known fairy tale fairly closely. Angelina (Cinderella) is ill-treated by her father, Don Magnifico, and her two step-sisters. Prince Ramiro, in search of a wife, swops places with his valet and falls in love with her at first sight. The Prince's tutor, Alidora (instead of a fairy godmother) helps Angelina attend the ball. Her identity is revealed finally by a silver bracelet.

Johann Strauss

Die Fledermaus

First produced in Vienna in 1872, *Die Fledermaus* (The Bat) was Strauss's great opera success. Baron von Eisenstein, about to go to prison for five days, is persuaded by Falke to go instead to a ball at Prince Orlofsky's. Meanwhile Rosalinda, Eisentein's wife, is visited by Alfred. When Frank, the prison governor comes to take the Baron to gaol, Alfred pretends to be him. Rosalinda then goes to the ball masked, where her husband flirts with her outrageously. All is cleared up next day at the prison.

Die Zigeunerbaron (The Gypsy Baron)

Strauss here takes a typically complicated and irreverent story and combines it with delightful melodies and occasionally adventurous orchestral writing to create a wholly entertaining work.

Richard Strauss

Der Rosenkavalier

The highpoint of Strauss's musical career, *Der Rosenkavalier,* with a libretto by the poet Hugo von Hofmannsthal, was first put on at Dresden in 1911. The Marschallin has been having an affair with young Octavian when Baron Ochs arrives, seeking a Rose Cavalier to carry a silver rose to his fiancée Sophie. Octavian finally takes it to her and they fall in love. After various twists, the Baron is hideously compromised in a tavern by Octavian, dressed as a maid, and is forced to let Sophie marry him.

Salome

Strauss's third opera and his first great success, *Salome's* libretto was translated by Lachmann from Wilde's drama and opened in Dresden in 1905. During a banquet Jokanaan (John the Baptist) proclaims the coming of the Messiah from the cistern where he is imprisoned. Brought out for Salome to see, he repels her fascinated advances and warns her against following the sinful ways of her mother, Herodias. He is then returned to the cistern and Herod, the Tetrarch, asks Salome to dance. Salome then dances the Dance of the Seven Veils, and demands her reward – Jokanaan's head. This she fondles until Herod, in disgust, tells his soldiers to crush her.

Ariadne auf Naxos

In its final version, produced in Vienna in 1916, with a text by Hofmannsthal after Molière, this features an opera within the opera, set in 18th-century Vienna. An idealist composer learns to his horror that his *opera seria (Ariadne)* is to accompany a *commedia dell-arte* performance. The latter in fact constantly disrupts the former, juxtaposing the comic and the tragic.

Capriccio

Strauss's last opera, first performed in Munich in 1942, with a libretto by Krauss and the composer, is set in 18th-century Paris. It concerns a Countess being wooed by two suitors – the poet Oliver and the composer Flamand, who argue whether music or words are of greater importance in opera. At the end the outcome seems unresolved, the last scene showing the Countess being about to announce her decision, but the golden autumnal beauty of the score suggests that music will win, though poetry still stands some chance.

Verdi

La Traviata

First performed in Venice in 1853, *La Traviata* (The Wayward One) has a text by Piave based on the novel *La Dame Aux Camelias* by Alexandre Dumas the Younger. Alfredo Germont falls in love with the beautiful courtesan Violetta Valery and persuades her to come and live with him on his country estate. Alfredo's father, however, visits her and persuades her to give up Alfredo: his daughter's engagement is threatened by the scandal of Alfredo's relationship. She agrees to make the sacrifice and returns to her former life. Alfredo, unaware of this, publicly insults Violetta at a ball. He learns the truth too late; Violetta dies in his arms from tuberculosis.

Aida

Reputedly written for the opening of the Suez Canal, Verdi's opera was not in fact first performed in Cairo until 1871. The libretto is by Ghislanzonie and Verdi after a plot by Bey. It is a story of war between Egypt and Ethiopia and the love of Radames, the captain of the guard, for Aida, daughter of the Ethiopian king and a slave at the Egyptian court. Tricked into betraying military secrets, Radames is condemned to be buried alive by the jealous fury of Amneris, an Egyptian princess, who also loves him. Aida, although she has escaped, prefers to die with him in his tomb. Meanwhile Amneris, who has also loved Radamis but in vain, prays for him as he dies.

Rigoletto

Verdi's first mature opera, *Rigoletto,* with a libretto by Piave after Hugo's drama *Le roi s'amuse,* produced in Venice in 1851. The lecherous Duke of Mantua has been courting Gilda while in disguise. Unknown to him, she is the daughter of his court-jester Rigoletto. When Rigoletto, who has unwittingly helped in the abduction of Gilda, learns the Duke has seduced her, he plans his assassination by Sparafucile. Sparafucile's sister begs him not to do the deed and is overheard by Gilda. She decides to substitute herself in order to save the life of her lover and dies in his place.

Il Trovatore

The four-act opera (The Troubadour) with a libretto by Cammarano after a play by Gutierrez opened in Rome in 1853. The notoriously confused plot takes place in 15th-century Spain during the revolt of the Count of Urgel against the King of Aragon. It involves gypsies, witches, counts, knights, a troubadour, nuns, cases of mistaken identity and of suicide, plots of murder and revenge all in quick succession. It remains a favourite among Verdi's operas.

Falstaff

Stimulated by the success of *Otello,* Verdi turned again to Shakespeare, starting work when he was over 75. Boito was again his librettist, combining parts of *The Merry Wives of Windsor* with *Henry IV* (part 1) to create a work superior to the original. It breaks new ground by almost cutting out traditional formal designs. *Falstaff* is one of the great comedies, funny yet also compassionate in characterization, showing a detachment possible only to the old in its final fugue 'All the world's a comedy'. It was Verdi's last opera.

La Forza del Destino

With a libretto by Piave after the drama *Don Alvaro* by the Duke of Rivas, it was first produced at St Petersburg in 1862. Don Alvaro, the hero, accidentally kills the father of his beloved, Leonora. Don Carlo, her brother, pursues Don Alvaro, seeking vengeance, while she shelters in a monastery. The two men meet in a battle and, not recognizing each other, become friends. But in the end Don Carlo and his sister both die, leaving Alvaro to destiny.

Otello

Towards the end of his life, Verdi came out of what had been a virtual retirement since composing his great *Requiem* in 1874 to write two last great operas based on plays by Shakespeare. With Boito proving his best-ever librettist, *Otello* actually improves on Shakespeare's play, being the finest of all Italian Romantic operas. The libretto is taut, the music, while not ignoring traditional forms, makes them infinitely serviceable in projecting the drama. The orchestra is used to maintain continuity, but does not diminish the importance of the voice. It received an enthusiastic first night in Milan in 1887. At first Verdi intended to call the opera *Iago,* because of the musical and dramatic importance he gave that role. Iago's 'Credo' in Act 2, where he expounds his philosophy of evil, rivals any of Shakespeare's soliloquies. In fact, the opera follows the play's outlines quite closely, and offers a superb opportunity for any great lyrical tenor in the title role.

Simon Boccanegra

This opera was no great success when it was first produced in 1857. But it must have remained close to Verdi's heart as, over 20 years later, he revised it extensively, creating the fine work we have today. Though in many ways it is a stark and gloomy opera, full of foreboding and Machiavellian deeds, it is also a work of tremendous vitality. The plot centres round the clashes between two rival political groups where Boccanegra becomes the victim of both betrayal and unjust insult. With Verdi's improved score, together with his marvellously sympathetic portrayal of the central character of Simon, this opera makes very worthy listening.

Don Carlos

Commissioned from Verdi by the Paris Opera, Don Carlos is the great culmination of Verdi's concern with politics, statesmanship, intrigue and the 'Ship of State'. It has a series of unforgettable portrayals, such as King Philip II, Elisabeth and Don Carlos himself, and in the opera, first performed in 1867, Verdi reached new operatic heights. It is certainly an ambitious work, dealing with its six principal figures and a whole range of themes – centring mainly on the forbidden love of Don Carlos and Elizabeth, who is betrothed to his father, Philip II. Don Carlos also contains an astonishingly varied musical score which successfully encompasses so many parallel threads. There is, besides, the usual power and beauty of Verdi's music which make the opera a veritable Italian feast.

Wagner

The Ring

This immense cycle of four operas needs three days and a preliminary evening, which is exceptional. The operas were composed as follows: (1) *Das Rheingold* (The Rhine Gold) first performed Munich, 1869; (2) *The Walkure* (The Valkyrie) first performed Munich, 1870; (3) *Siegfried* first performed Bayreuth 1876; (4) *Götterdämmerung* (Twilight of the Gods) first performed Bayreuth, 1876. Wagner's own libretto was based on the Nibelung saga. The plots concern the theft of a ring by the gods and the attempts by Wotan and others to regain it, despite the curse laid on it. In the end, the ring returns to the Rhine maidens and Valhalla ends in flames. The work is a timeless drama about power and corruption.

Die Meistersinger von Nürnberg

Wagner's only comedy, with his own libretto as usual, was first performed in Munich in 1868. Walther falls in love with Eva but discovers her father has promised her to the winner of the singing contest to be held shortly. Walther dreams a great song and sings it to Sachs, the cobbler. But Beckmester, his rival, steals the song to sing at the contest. He sings it so badly that everyone laughs; then Walther sings to win the prize and Eva's hand, which he accepts after Sachs explains the Meistersingers' purpose.

Tristan und Isolde

First performed in Munich in 1865, its libretto was adapted by Wagner from ancient legends. Tristan loves Isolde. She is compelled to marry King Mark of Cornwall and orders Brangane to prepare poison for her and Tristan. But Brangane substitutes a love potion for them so they become aware of their love. While Mark is away, Tristan and Isolde meet and sing of their love before King Mark returns to surprise them. In the fight that follows Tristan is badly wounded and taken to Brittany. Isolde finally follows him but Tristan is so excited he tears off his bandages and dies, to be followed by Isolde.

Parsifal

First performed in Bayreuth in 1882, this was Wagner's last opera, called by him a 'sacred festival drama'. It relates how Amfortas, a Knight of the Holy Grail, has been seduced by Kundry and wounded by the evil magician Klingsor. Parsifal, a holy innocent, finally manages to regain the lost lance and so heal Amfortas, becoming King of the Knights in his place.

Glossary of operatic terms

A

added numbers Songs or arias by other composers inserted into operas by singers wishing to display their vocal abilities and not worried about disturbing the flow of the opera.

antefatto Italian for 'antecedent fact'. An introduction, usually written in a libretto but sometimes sung at the beginning of an opera, giving information about events preceding the opera. Sometimes resembles a prologue before the main action of a play begins.

arioso Section of recitative, sung with more expression than usual, more in aria style.

B

boccha chiusa Italian for 'closed mouth'. Basically humming. Often used in teaching or learning roles but sometimes the direction in a score to singers.

'Breeches role' *See* travesty.

brindisi Italian for 'drinking song'. Special composition of recognizable but high quality arias encouraging others to drink.

C

cabaletta From Italian for 'extraction'. Usually refers to the second part of an aria in two sections, the first being slower, the second a brilliant passage, quick, with repeats, sometimes with the singer's own embellishments.

cadenza From Italian for 'cadence' or 'final flourish'. Originally, elaborate improvisation by singers in certain arias, becoming progressively more brilliant. This became increasingly common practice, and composers who feared their singers might go too far would, for safety's sake, write their own cadenzas.

cantilena From Italian for 'cradle song'. Description of gentle flowing melody or tune, or instruction for singing a certain passage in this way.

canzonetta From Italian for 'song'. Light, simple solo song.

cavatina From Italian for 'carved out'. Short, simple arias of one lyrical section. Sometimes the first part of an aria of which cabaletta is the second.

cercar la nota Italian for 'to search for the note'. The practise of anticipating the next note by singing a light middle note, or gently singing the next note before rendering it at the correct volume.

colla voce Italian for 'with the voice'. Instruction for orchestra or instruments accompanying the singer to play with exactly the same tempo, pitch and phrasing.

coloratura Brilliant ornamentation of the vocal line, light, agile, sparkling. This term is also sometimes used to describe a soprano specializing in singing in this way. Is rarely, but can sometimes be used prejoratively.

comprimario Italian for 'with the principal'. Singer supporting the principal singers but with little individuality.

couplet Song of several verses each sung to the same tune. Often lighter and much used in operetta.

covered tone A soft, gentle voice quality capable of great beauty and intensity, as found in the works of many great composers.

D

deus ex machina Latin for 'the god from the machine'. Originally, a technique for lowering a god on to a cloud at the end of opera, now a phrase also used to describe an easy solution to a complex plot, or a plot generally lacking direction.

E

encore French for 'again'. Command used by English-speaking audiences calling for repeat of a popular or well-sung aria (Italians and French use 'bis').

entr'acte Small piece of purely orchestral music played either between scenes with the curtain lowered for a scene change, or between acts. The 'Sea Interlude' in Benjamin Britten's *Peter Grimes* are a famous example.

L

lamento A tragic aria common in classical Italian operas placed before the resolution of the plot, usually to give a weighty contrast to the happy ending.

leitmotiv German for 'leading motiv'. Partly used by Weber but thoroughly employed by Wagner in most of his operas, especially in the *Ring* cycle. Basically, signature tunes for characters, like Siegfried, or ideas, like The Curse, but subtly changed with moods and emotions, often creating a subconscious awareness of the intricacies of the score.

M

messa di voce Italian for 'placing of voice'. Technique more used in bel canto era for placing crescendos and diminuendos on a single note. Popular because it shows great skill.

music drama A favourite phrase of Wagner, who placed great store by the unity of all the arts used in opera – music, drama, painting, singing – rather than allowing opera to be merely a vehicle for vocal display.

P

parlando Italian for 'speaking'. Instruction to let the voice adopt the style of speech in certain recitative passages rather than singing normally.

patter song Song using large number of words produced at a rapid rate. Usually comic and best seen in the works of Gilbert and Sullivan. These, however, are parodies of a style found in Haydn, Mozart and bel canto composers. Leporello's 'Catalogue Aria' in Don Giovanni is an early example.

S

sotto voce Italian for 'below the voice'. Instructions to use soft voice in certain passages.

soubrette From French for cunning. Secondary soprano character with some personality and wit, often a servant girl.

spieltenor German for 'acting tenor'. Tenor specializing in German comic roles where a large amount of dialogue and acting ability is called for.

spinto Italian for 'pushed'. Voice between lyric and dramatic tenor.

stretta Italian for 'squeezing'. The speeding up of a passage, either aria or ensemble, to make an exciting climax, usually at the end of an act.

sprechgesang German for 'speech song'. Type of speech which is notated, that is, has to be on exact notes. It falls between speech and song and was much used by Schoenberg and his followers. It is not the same as recitative (see page 75). Humperdinck used the technique as early as his Königsbinder in 1897.

T

tessitura Italian for 'texture'. Average range of character's voice in an opera, e.g. certain soprano roles are said to have a high tessitura.

travesty From French for disguise. 'Breeches role' where male characters are sung by women. One of the most famous examples is that of Octavian (a soprano or mezzo) in Richard Strauss's *Der Rosenkavalier*.

V

vibrato Italian for 'vibrated'. Method of sustaining a note in an interesting way by rising above it rapidly. The wavering of pitch can be used to intensify voice or strings.

W

Wagner tuba Instrument developed by Wagner to lie between horns and trumpets. Usually played by horn players, there are four of them, two tenors and two basses.

Index

Bibliography

J. Anthony, *French Baroque Music from Beaujoyeulx to Rameau,* Norton, New York, 1981

L. Bernstein, *Bernstein on Broadway,* Schirmer Books, New York, 1981

L. Biancolli (ed), *Opera Reader,* Greenwood, Westport, 1977

A. Blyth, *Opera on Record,* Longwood Publishing Group, Dover, 1984

N. Broder, *Samuel Barber,* Greenwood, Westport, 1985

M. Brown (ed), *Mussorgsky: In Memoriam 1881–1981,* UMI Press, Ann Arbor, 1982

R. Clarson Leach, *Berlioz: His Life and Times,* Hippocrene Books, New York, 1984

M. Cooper, *Georges Bizet,* Greenwood, Westport, 1971

W. Croxten, *French Grand Opera: An Art and a Business,* Da Capo, New York, 1972

R. Davis, *Opera in Chicago,* Irvington Press, New York, 1986

R. Donnington, *The Opera,* Harcourt House, London, 1981

J. Drummond, *Opera in Perspective,* University of Minnesota Press, Minneapolis, 1980

Q. Eaton, *Opera,* Abaris Books, New York, 1980

R. Englander, *Opera? What's all the Screaming About?* Walker and Co, New York, 1983

G. Flaherty, *Opera in the Development of German Critical Thought,* University of Princeton Press, Princeton, 1978

R. Freeman, *Opera without Drama: Concepts of Change in Italian Opera 1675–1725,* UMI Press, Ann Arbor, 1981

H. Graf, *Opera for the People,* Da Capo, New York, 1973

C. Hamm, *Opera,* Da Capo, New York, 1980

R. Holloway, *Debussy and Wagner,* Da Capo, New York, 1982

I. Holst, *Britten,* Faber and Faber, London, 1980

P. Howard, *Gluck and the Birth of Modern Opera,* Cambridge University Press, Cambridge, 1981

C. Kobbe, *Complete Opera Book,* Random House, New York, 1956

R. Lieberman, *Opera Years,* Riverrun, New York, 1985

H. Lindenberger, *Opera: The Extravagant Art,* Cornell University Press, Ithaca, 1984

G. Martin, *Verdi: His Music, Life and Times,* Da Capo, New York, 1979

P. Masson, *Opera de Rameau,* Da Capo, New York, 1972

W. McSpadden, *Opera Synopses: A Guide to the Plots and Characters of the Standard Opera,* Folcroft Library Editions, Darby, 1978

E. Mordden, *Opera Anecdotes,* Oxford University Press, Oxford, 1985

E. Newmann, *The Wagner Operas* (2 vols), Harper and Row, New York, 1983

L. Orrey, *Opera in the High Baroque,* Riverrun, New York, 1981

G. Perle, *The Operas of Alban Berg: (i) Wozzek (ii) Lulu,* Univerity of California Press, Berkeley, 1984

P. Pettit, *Verdi,* Riverrun, New York, 1981

H. Pleasants, *The Great Singers,* Fireside Books, New York, 1985

H. Rosenthal, *Opera* (5 vols), Da Capo, New York, 1979

P. Robinson, *Opera and Ideas: From Mozart to Strauss,* Harper and Row, New York, 1985

C. Schwartz, *Gershwin: His Life and Music,* Da Capo, New York, 1979

N. Sorkina, *Prokofiev,* Paganiniana Publishing, Neptune, 1984

R. Southwell-Sander, *Verdi: His Life and Times,* Hippocrene Books, New York, 1978

N. Till, *Rossini: His Life and Times,* Hippocrene Books, New York, 1983

J. Westrup, *Purcell,* J. M. Dent, London, 1975

E. White, *Stravinsky: A Critical Study,* Greenwood, Westport, Connecticut, 1979

S. Worsthorne, *Venetian Opera in the 17th Century,* Da Capo, New York, 1984